STEVEN CANNY

Steven Canny is an executive producer and writer who has spent a surprisingly long period of time making television, theatre and radio.

Theatre work includes *The Arthur Conan Doyle Appreciation Society* (Traverse Theatre); *No Wise Men* (Liverpool Playhouse); *Origins* (Theatre Severn); *Spyski* (Lyric Hammersmith); *The Hound of the Baskervilles* (Duchess Theatre). Steven was Associate Director at Complicité for five years where he made theatre across the world and then worked with Al Pacino on *The Resistible Rise of Arturo Ui*.

Television producing includes *Two Doors Down*, *Still Game*, *Mammoth*, *Mrs Brown's Boys*, *Jonathan Creek*, *Porridge*, *Bob Servant*, *The Tuckers*, *A Christmas Carol Goes Wrong*, Kieran Hodgson's *How We Forgot to Save the Planet*.

Steven also produced and directed drama and comedy for radio including BBC Radio 4's *News Quiz* and has adapted a number of pieces for radio including *A Shropshire Lad* with Simon Russell Beale which then played at the National Theatre and Complicité's *Mnemonic* for BBC Radio 3.

His recent shows have won BAFTA, National Television Award, Scottish BAFTA, IFTA, RTS Scotland, TV Times Award, Celtic Media and Sony Golds.

JOHN NICHOLSON

John Nicholson is an Artistic Director of the award-winning Peepolykus, with whom he has toured the UK and the world for twenty-five years.

Writing includes *The Hound of the Baskervilles* (Leeds Playhouse/West End/national tour); *No Wise Men* (Liverpool Everyman & Playhouse); *Treasure Island* (Bristol Old Vic/national tour); *The Massive Tragedy of Madame Bovary* (Northampton Royal/national tour); *A Christmas Carol* (Exeter Northcott); *Spyski – The Importance of Being Honest* (Lyric Hammersmith/national tour); *The Ramsbury Players* (National Theatre); *Richard's Rampage* (The Old Vic/international tour); *Origins* (Pentabus/national tour); *The Arthur Conan Doyle Appreciation Society* (Traverse Theatre); *Help! Get Me Out of This Musical* (South Hill Park); *A Trespasser's Guide to the Classics series 1 and 2, Rik Mayall's Bedside Tales series 1, Marley Was Dead* (BBC Radio 4); *Off Their Rockers* (ITV).

Physical comedy director/consultant credits include *One Man, Two Guvnors* (Bolton Octagon/national tour); *A Little Hotel on the Side* (Theatre Royal Bath); *The Secret Adversary* (Watermill, Newbury); *Watson and Oliver, The Wrong Door* (BBC); *Playtime* (Northampton Royal); *Accidental Death of an Anarchist* (Sheffield Theatres).

Directing credits include *Partners in Crime* (Queens Theatre, Hornchurch); *Dracula: The Bloody Truth, 400* (Plymouth Theatre Royal/National); *Shaun The Sheep Live* (Aardman/international); *Nina Conti – Dolly Mixtures* (Soho Theatre/West End); *Paul Merton – Out Of His Head* (West End); *Spymonkey's Spook Show* (Blackpool Winter Gardens); *Coulrophobia* (London International Mime Festival); *Aladdin, Dick Tracy* (Plymouth Athenaeum); *The Three Musketeers* (York Theatre Royal/national tour); *King Arthur* (national tour); *The Light Princess* (Tobacco Factory Theatre, Bristol); *A Christmas Carol* (Exeter Northcott).

Steven Canny & John Nicholson

THE TIME MACHINE

A Comedy

(*Very loosely*) *adapted from the novel by H. G. Wells*

NICK HERN BOOKS
London
www.nickhernbooks.co.uk

A Nick Hern Book

The Time Machine first published in Great Britain in 2023 as a paperback original by Nick Hern Books Limited, The Glasshouse, 49a Goldhawk Road, London W12 8QP

The Time Machine copyright © 2023 Steven Canny and John Nicholson

Steven Canny and John Nicholson have asserted their moral right to be identified as the authors of this work

Cover image: Rebecca Pitt

Designed and typeset by Nick Hern Books, London
Printed in the UK by Mimeo Ltd, Huntingdon, Cambridgeshire PE29 6XX

A CIP catalogue record for this book is available from the British Library

ISBN 978 1 83904 296 6

CAUTION All rights whatsoever in this play are strictly reserved. Requests to reproduce the text in whole or in part should be addressed to the publisher.

Amateur Performing Rights Applications for performance, including readings and excerpts, by amateurs in English should be addressed to the Performing Rights Manager, Nick Hern Books, The Glasshouse, 49a Goldhawk Road, London W12 8QP, *tel* +44 (0)20 8749 4953, *email* rights@nickhernbooks.co.uk, except as follows:

Australia: ORiGiN Theatrical, *email* enquiries@originmusic.com.au, *web* www.origintheatrical.com.au

New Zealand: Play Bureau, 20 Rua Street, Mangapapa, Gisborne, 4010, *tel* +64 21 258 3998, *email* info@playbureau.com

Professional Performing Rights Applications for performance by professionals in any medium and in any language throughout the world should be addressed, in the first instance, to Nick Hern Books, see details above.

No performance of any kind may be given unless a licence has been obtained. Applications should be made before rehearsals begin. Publication of this play does not necessarily indicate its availability for amateur performance.

www.nickhernbooks.co.uk/environmental-policy

The Time Machine was first performed at New Wolsey Theatre, Ipswich, on 23 February 2023, before touring the UK and transferring to Park Theatre, London, on 30 November 2023. The cast was as follows:

ACTORS	Michael Dylan
	Dave Hearn
	Amy Revelle
Director	Orla O'Loughlin
Designer	Fred Meller
Lighting Designer	Colin Grenfell
Sound Designer	Greg Clarke
Props Supervisor	Katie Balmforth
Costume Supervisor	Federica Romano

Acknowledgements

Our experience is that a new play is the positive result of an act of faith engaged in by many, many, people. We're indebted to our friend Mark Shanahan for the early research and development. We're also very grateful to Original Theatre for their support and encouragement. Lots of people made positive contributions in the development process but the people we owe most to are the original cast and director. Amy, Michael, Dave and Orla have committed time, love, energy, imagination and their collective pleasure in – and understanding of – making people laugh. They've interrogated when things were half-baked, always asked meaningful questions and have offered generous and thoughtful solutions to problems that have caused us bellyaches and headaches. Making people laugh is such a pleasure and a privilege and we're incredibly lucky to have had the chance to do this with people we love and cherish. And if the play doesn't make you laugh… well, it's obviously all those other people to blame! Thanks for reading.

S.C. and J.N.

For our dads

Characters

ACTOR 1, *Michael*
ACTOR 2, *Amy*
ACTOR 3, *Dave*

The actors also play:

LADY GRETA ZSA ZSA ZSA
DR EVAN BINKLEY
FRANK FROM EASTENDERS
PAT BUTCHER FROM EASTENDERS
MISS PIGGY
KERMIT
MEGHAN MARKLE
PRINCE HARRY
QUEEN VICTORIA
FILBY
MRS RICHARDS
MARY SELBY
WELLS
WEENA
MORLOCK

This text went to press before the end of rehearsals and so may differ slightly from the play as performed.

Note on Text

We will learn that Amy, Michael and Dave have created many shows together. This is their new offering and, production-wise, they've scaled up. However, since they've thrown all the budget at the set, responsibility for operating technical aspects of the show remains in their hands. Future casts should use their own names.

If something has gone wrong within a scene, a dialogue line might be attributed to the actor's name rather than the character they're playing. So in effect, they should play this line as themselves, not the character. Ideally, a plant is required to play a front-of-house person and a pizza-delivery person (although it might be possible to use theatre staff). The people brought up on stage in Act Two however should be genuine (unknowing) audience members.

Where there is a reference/jokes around specific locations, or cultural references that won't 'read' outside of the UK, please feel free to make adjustments accordingly and run them by the authors.

ACT ONE

Pre-set: USR: a chaise longue covered with a sheet (black tat), behind it, a small table with a tray of tea, a stand for a plant. USL: a drinks trolley covered with a sheet (black tat), a set of steps.

Scene One – Introductions

Music, swirling lights and smoke ('Immigrant Song' by Led Zeppelin or 'Step on Up' by Rockin' For Decades). After a few seconds the announcement begins.

DAVE (*over music*). Esteemed audience members, welcome to this wonderful theatre. Prepare to be amazed and please welcome to the stage, Dave –

The announcement and music cuts. Pause. MICHAEL appears (in rehearsal-room clothes).

MICHAEL. Please just bear with us.

Music/announcement immediately restarts.

DAVE (*over music*). Esteemed audience members, welcome to this wonderful theatre. Prepare to be amazed and please welcome to the stage, Dave –

Announcement and music cuts again. MICHAEL enters again and straight off the back of this...

MICHAEL. Right, well that's all gone tits up. Hello.

He has a laptop (that runs the show). AMY appears (in rehearsal-room clothes), upbeat. MICHAEL is pressing keys.

AMY (*bold, keeping energy up*). But no worries, hello, because sometimes a challenge can become an opportunity.

MICHAEL (*distracted*). Yes.

AMY. For a song.

ACT ONE, SCENE ONE 11

MICHAEL. No!

AMY (*big announcement*). So while we resolve this technical issue… London, this is 'Believe' by the global icon, Cher!

DAVE (*off*). No it isn't!

DAVE *bursts in, also in rehearsal-room clothes.*

Ha, ha! Thank you, Amy, but an a cappella Cher song will thankfully not be necessary. (*To audience.*) Rest assured, we're now back on track. Are we?

MICHAEL (*tapping keys*). I'm not exactly sure what's –

DAVE. There we go. Esteemed audience members, tonight you will bear witness to a startling and alarming revelation about H. G. Wells's *The Time Machine* that will change the way you view the world. For ever. Now, I appreciate that most of you will have come here tonight expecting to be entertained. You need to let that thought go. My name is –

'Immigrant Song' kicks back in.

MICHAEL. We're sorted. Sorry, Dave.

DAVE. No, leave it on, it works. My name is Dave Wells: actor, writer, director and intellectual adventurer. Dave… Wells!? A coincidence? No! Because I am in fact… actually turn it off, it's really distracting.

MICHAEL *cuts the music.*

Because I am in fact the great-great-grandson of Herbert George Wells himself.

MICHAEL. Aka H. G. Wells.

DAVE. Yes indeed.

AMY. You can close your mouth, sir.

MICHAEL. The resemblance is actually uncanny.

DAVE. This is Amy Tymes – actress.

AMY. Actor. And singer.

DAVE. And this is Michael O'Reilly – just actor.

MICHAEL. And company tour booker.

DAVE. They don't need to know that. People of Finsbury Park –

MICHAEL. And other London boroughs.

DAVE. Until a matter of weeks ago…

A few pieces of confetti flutter down from the flies. They all clock this.

Until a matter of weeks ago, the world had assumed that H. G. Wells's seminal time-travelling novel was a work of fiction. But no. We can reveal that it is in fact –

MICHAEL. Fact.

DAVE. Fact.

AMY. The events described within the book…

MICHAEL. Are real.

DAVE. Are real!

A theatre lamp blows and sounds real. A believable but augmented ting. They all look up. It's obviously a bit darker.

(*To the audience.*) Sorry, a light just blew. Is that safe?

MICHAEL. It's just a patching issue with the LED. It's fine.

DAVE. Is it?

MICHAEL. It's been PAT tested.

DAVE. Who's Pat?

AMY. Just carry on.

DAVE. Now. I'm not expecting you to comprehend what I've just told you straight away.

MICHAEL. We certainly didn't.

AMY. Nope. Seemed like total bullsh–

DAVE. So… in order to convince you of the truth, we need to begin at the beginning.

MICHAEL *starts pushing the covered chaise longue from SL to SR in front of the covered drinks trolley.*

ACT ONE, SCENE TWO 13

AMY. A community centre near Ealing where we were rehearsing *The Importance of Being Earnest* – the show we'd actually, properly, rehearsed and were supposed to be performing here this week.

DAVE. But all that changed when I walked into rehearsals carrying a cardboard box.

MICHAEL. This was the moment our lives changed for ever.

DAVE brings on a free-standing door from the USR wing and places it USR. A sign that reads 'rehearsal room' hangs on it. AMY *grabs a script,* MICHAEL *grabs props.*

DAVE. And so that is the moment we must recreate for you first. Please be aware that everything you will see from now on is true. As it happened.

MICHAEL. This is verbatim theatre!

AMY. Using the actual words we used.

DAVE. More or less.

AMY. The actual words. With no extemporising by one of us in particular to make himself look good.

DAVE. Whatever. And action! (*He hides behind the door.*)

Scene Two – Rehearsal One

MICHAEL *and* AMY *are sitting on the chaise longue, rehearsing.*

MICHAEL (*reading*). 'I am known for the gentleness of my disposition and the extraordinary sweetness of my nature. But I warn you...'

He drops out of character on AMY*'s look.*

What?

AMY. Just talk normally. It's not panto.

MICHAEL. 'From the moment I saw you I distrusted you. I felt that you were false and deceitful.'

AMY. What? What's brought this on? Is this still about the awkward sex we had on tour?

MICHAEL. What?! No, that's all Oscar Wilde. And what do you mean, *awkward*?

AMY. Do you really want to discuss this now?

MICHAEL. Yes.

AMY. Okay, well firstly I hadn't planned on wearing such a tight-fitting top...

DAVE *bursts in with a box.*

MICHAEL. Where have you been?

AMY. And why are you sweating so aggressively?

DAVE *produces a manuscript.*

DAVE. You remember me telling you that my family's been asked to donate all my great-great-grandfather's papers to the British Library? Well get this.

He kneels in front of them. Lights change. They all freeze. Very brief, fun, time-passing music effect until the music stops and they unfreeze.

MICHAEL *and* AMY. 'Kin' 'ell.

DAVE (*to the audience*). What I revealed to them was that this is the original, ink-scribbled manuscript for H. G. Wells's *The Time Machine*.

A phone rings in the audience. It's the USHER*'s. He/she exits to take the call.*

It was discovered in a locked box in my auntie's attic, along with other personal items – H. G. Wells's shaving mirror and this beautiful knife he kept on his desk...

AMY. No, I think that's the prop knife for the Morlock scene later.

MICHAEL *stabs his hand with the retractable/trick blade.*

ACT ONE, SCENE TWO 15

MICHAEL. They must have got mixed up.

DAVE. So the one-of-a-kind antique knife is just sitting on the props table?

MICHAEL. It's fine. I'll switch them back later.

DAVE. Amy, my chair please. Here we go.

AMY *fetches an office chair on wheels*. DAVE *sits*.

MICHAEL. Prepare to have your minds well and truly bended.

DAVE. Bent. Within these pages are detailed descriptions of events that took place *after* my great-great-grandfather had died! But it doesn't stop there. Exhibit One.

AMY. A hundred-year-old photo of Dave Chisnall winning the 2023 darts Players Championship.

DAVE. Dated in Wells's unmistakable handwriting! Go ahead, Michael. Pass it around… that's enough, it's priceless. Exhibit Two.

AMY. One concert ticket.

DAVE. For a Take That reunion tour featuring Robbie Williams in 2025!

MICHAEL. Yes London, you heard it here first.

DAVE. And finally. Exhibit Three. Amy, will you please read out the letter from Mr William Heinemann, H. G. Wells's publisher.

AMY. 'Dear Mr Wells. I fear you have lost control of your senses. Your journal entries suggesting, for example; "an era of flower power" seventy years from now in the 1960s, are utterly ridiculous.'

DAVE. A lucky shot-in-the-dark prediction? Clearly not. Now. For those of you who haven't read the published version of *The Time Machine* – and, frankly, I'm appalled and disappointed in you – it describes how the human species evolves eight hundred thousand years into the future –

MICHAEL. Trigger warning: it's not pretty.

DAVE. No – not unless we make significant changes to our behaviour.

He gets up from his chair and all three start to walk forwards.

People of Finsbury Park –

MICHAEL. Finsbury Parkers.

DAVE. What?

MICHAEL. That's what they call themselves.

DAVE. Really?! Okay.

They repeat the movement.

Finsbury Parkers.

MICHAEL. And boroughs beyond.

DAVE (*trying to control his irritation*). *The Time Machine* is not merely a prophetic warning. It's a first-hand account of a future we're currently setting the foundations for. Question, Amy.

AMY. I do. Have one. So, why didn't H. G. Wells make this public during his lifetime?

DAVE. Because he would have been branded a lunatic…

MICHAEL. A crackhead.

AMY. Pot.

MICHAEL. Pothead.

DAVE. No.

MICHAEL. Potcrack.

DAVE. Try again.

MICHAEL. Crackpot!

DAVE. There it is. It was clearly incumbent on us – as actors – to dramatise the truth about how our species is destined to evolve if we fail to take action. This is what happened next.

AMY. The rehearsal room, the following day.

Scene Three – Dave Convinces His Fellow Actors

DAVE. So, we deliver my great-great-grandfather's message in a bottle that never went to sea.

AMY. Dave!

DAVE. We can even use the chair he used for lecture tours.

AMY. Dave!! Are you seriously suggesting we contact *every single* theatre that's booked *The Importance of Being Earnest* – how many's that, Michael?

MICHAEL. One.

AMY. One?!

MICHAEL. Oh, and Lumpton Marsh Village Hall are a yes if we run an over-sixty-fives' movement workshop – (*He gives a hopeful thumbs up.*)

AMY. ...*all* of those theatres, and tell them we want to replace our presentation of arguably the most enduring of British comedies with a book where not a lot really happens.

DAVE. 'Not a lot really happens'?!

AMY. Action-wise.

DAVE. He travels through time, Amy. How much more action do you want? And it's all true!

AMY. But Dave, will this evidence alone really convince discerning theatregoers?

MICHAEL. It will in Lumpton Marsh.

AMY. But a cultural hub like Wolverhampton? Or Finsbury Park?

MICHAEL. Love the Park Theatre – such a friendly and sophisticated audience.

DAVE. No, Amy, you're right. We'll need more. Testimonials, eyewitness accounts, anything we can get a hold of.

MICHAEL. Let's do this. And so we began an extensive period of verification.

   MICHAEL *pushes the plant stand backstage.*

Scene Four – Research

DAVE *wheels himself to the door and turns the rehearsal-room sign around to read: 'Verification HQ', and dials a mobile. He gets out of time with the SFX keyboard sounds. An old house phone rings.* AMY *appears USL.*

LADY ZSA ZSA ZSA. Lady Greta Zsa Zsa Zsa.

DAVE. Lady Zsa Zsa Zsa, this is Dave Wells. H. G. Wells's great-great-grandson.

LADY ZSA ZSA ZSA. What can I do for you, sugar?

DAVE. You say that you remember your mother telling you that she remembers *her* mother, your grandmother, telling her that she remembers *her* mother – your mother's grandmother, telling her that she remembers H. G. Wells turning up at her door and proposing to her *after* he had died.

LADY ZSA ZSA ZSA. Yes, that is all true, darling!

She hangs up.

DAVE (*to the audience*). Proof! Case file two.

Another phone rings. MICHAEL *answers. Underscore of* The X Files.

DR BINKLEY. Dr Evan Binkley.

DAVE. The President of the Society for Historical Conspiracy Research? Is this a good time?

DR BINKLEY. No, I'm watching *The X Files*. Or as I like to call it – the real news. Who is this?

DAVE. This is Dave Wells, H. G. Wells's great-great-grandson.

DR BINKLEY. Well if your intention is to mock me… my career is in ruins after his visit here last year!

DAVE. A visit from H. G. Wells? Last year? Seventy-three years after he had died?

DR BINKLEY. Look, I didn't believe it at first. Not until he made me study the photographs. *But* the closer I looked, the clearer it became – often just the back of his head or a blurry chin, but at every significant historical event he's there…

AMY *holds up blown-up pictures*.

The World War One Christmas Day football truce – there right at the back. The fall of the Berlin Wall. An extra disciple at the Last Supper!

DAVE. We did ignore that last one. But more proof. And finally, Finsbury Park – don't say it, Michael – we have one more surprise for you. In town for one night only and here to confirm our findings, please put your hands together for the one, the only, Professor Brian Cox!

Pause. AMY *appears*.

AMY. He's not coming.

DAVE. What? Can we get him on the phone?

AMY. He's blocked all my calls.

DAVE. Amy, do we have anything?

AMY. We've got this.

MICHAEL *produces a life-sized cut-out of the celebrity physicist, Brian Cox.*

MICHAEL (*impression*). I'm Brian Cox.

DAVE. That'll do. Proof!

AMY. The further we looked, the more compelling the evidence became.

DAVE. I began the arduous but necessary dramatisation of the events my great-great-grandfather had witnessed. But interpreting his scribbles was no easy task.

MICHAEL. The rehearsal room, three weeks later.

Transition to rehearsal room.

DAVE (*on sitting*). Morning, guys. So you love my first draft, that's excellent.

MICHAEL. No, wait –

AMY. Verbatim theatre, Dave, we agreed. Exactly what was said…

DAVE. Fine! (*On sitting.*) Morning, guys. What do you mean, 'it's a piece of shit'?

MICHAEL. How on earth are we going to make the miniature time machine disappear in the parlour scene?

DAVE (*thinks*). Wait... hang on... got it! I'll create a revolving trap in the middle of a card table.

MICHAEL. Interesting.

AMY. Won't that just look like it's gone down a revolving trap in the middle of a card table?

DAVE. Trust me, audiences will be blown away!

AMY. Okay. And I see I'm basically just playing a scantily clad, futuristic dimwit for Wells to save, am I?

DAVE. Weena's not your only character, Amy.

AMY. Plus a non-appearing housemaid and his wedding-obsessed fiancée?

DAVE. Okay, I'll do another pass. But Wells didn't write many female characters.

MICHAEL. But he did write some pretty insightful dialogue.

AMY. So at least tap into that. And what about songs?

MICHAEL. I think he just stuck to novels?

AMY. I mean for the show! Where are the songs?

DAVE. Amy, we're delivering a message about planetary custodianship!

AMY. No Cher songs, no Amy. (*She begins to exit.*)

DAVE. Okay, one Cher song.

AMY. Five.

DAVE. Two.

AMY. Six.

DAVE. Wow. Okay, we'll talk about it.

MICHAEL. Actually, Dave, there is something important we've overlooked.

ACT ONE, SCENE FOUR   21

DAVE. Hit me up, big boy.

MICHAEL. A comprehensive flipchart presentation on the time-travel paradoxes.

AMY *laughs, then...*

AMY. Oh, God, he's not joking.

MICHAEL. Dave, without the science, no one will take us seriously. (*Pointing into auditorium.*) Trust me, there'll be cynics out there muttering to themselves 'H. G. Wells went to a Take That reunion concert in 2025? Poppycock! A talented props person made that ticket in Photoshop.'

AMY. Who the hell says poppycock?!

MICHAEL (*pointing*). Some of them might not even believe you're related to him!

DAVE. Idiots. Take a look at my face, people! Okay –

AMY. No. Don't weaken, Dave.

MICHAEL. Davey.

AMY. Dave.

MICHAEL. Daveyboy.

AMY. David!

DAVE. Amy... Michael's right. An understanding of the science was vital to Wells. If we skip that then there's a high risk our show will simply be remembered as... Oh I dunno...

MICHAEL. Two hours of utter nonsense.

DAVE. And I'll be *damned* if I'm gonna let that happen!

AMY. There'll be complaints.

MICHAEL. No one's going to complain!

Scene Five – An Explanation of Time-Travel Paradoxes

Lights change. Back to the present. MICHAEL *is setting up a flipchart and putting on a science lab coat, about to begin his lecture.*

DAVE. Due to complaints about Michael's paradox explanations –

MICHAEL. Hang on, what? From where?

AMY. Lumpton Marsh Village Hall.

MICHAEL. Well we're hardly taking Lumpton Marsh as representative! They only got the internet three years ago.

AMY *produces a letter and starts reading.*

AMY. 'Dear company, your time paradox explanations have driven my husband into a dark vortex of perceived missed opportunities. He's now living in the garden shed with a cardboard cut-out of Claudia Winkleman.' That's no laughing matter, Michael.

DAVE *is gathering the necessary props/costumes*

MICHAEL *(to* DAVE*).* And what do you think you're doing?

DAVE. We've been obliged to theatrically reimagine your presentation.

MICHAEL. Well you can nip that idea right in the butt, buddy.

DAVE. It's actually bud.

MICHAEL. Right in the butt bud… Bud butt…

DAVE. Almost.

MICHAEL. Butt buddy.

DAVE. No.

MICHAEL. You can nip that idea right in the bud, buddy.

DAVE. There we go. Don't worry, Michael, we've simply made the science more accessible. You know – jazzed things up a bit. All you need to do is introduce them. Alright, Paradox One. Let's go.

ACT ONE, SCENE FIVE   23

MICHAEL *turns the page on a flipchart. His complicated diagrams have titles above them.*

MICHAEL. The Grandfather Paradox.

SFX: EastEnders (*massive UK TV show set in East London*) *dramatic DUFF DUFF DUFF theme tune. Underscore establishes.* DAVE *enters as* FRANK (*a very recognisable character from the show*).

What's happening now?

FRANK. Pat? Pat?!

PAT (*off*). What'chu Brussels-sprouting about now, Frank?!

FRANK. Who'd ya get that flippin' time machine off've from?

AMY *enters as* PAT BUTCHER – *also a very recognisable character from the show – leopard-print coat, wig, cigarette and big hoop earrings.*

PAT. The Mitchell bruvvers. You got a problem with that?

FRANK. Nah. Course not, princess.

PAT. Good. Cos I'm gonna go back and witness the time my grandparents first met. Don't wait up.

DAVE *hits the laptop.* AMY *spins on the spot. Lights and sound signify time travel. We're on a train platform.*

Blimey, it's all so different a hundred years ago, or so. There's my young grandmother getting off the Walford steam flyer. And there's my young grandfather. They're about to have their chance meeting!

DAVE *sticks a hat on* MICHAEL *and a sign round his neck that reads 'Young Grandad'.*

FRANK. Oh, Friar Tuck me! What if Pat accidently stops her grandparents from meeting by distracting them or summat!?

PAT. Alright, sweetheart? After a bit of Posh 'n' Becks?

MICHAEL. What? Seriously? I'm your grandfather!?

PAT. Grandfather!

SFX: EastEnders *TV show dramatic DUFF DUFF DUFF theme tune.* AMY *exits.*

DAVE. Alright, thank you, Amy. On reflection, that probably needed a smidge more rehearsal. But the paradox being, that you could go back in time and apparently get off with your grandad and stop yourself from being born. Is that about the nub of it?

MICHAEL. Oh my God.

DAVE. Close enough. Alright, Paradox Two.

MICHAEL *turns the page on the flipchart.*

MICHAEL. The Hitler Paradox.

SFX: The Muppet Show *underscore.* AMY *enters with an upright bed (cloth on a stick).*

I'm so sorry. I really have no idea what is going on.

DAVE. Michael. Pillows. Now!

MICHAEL *stands behind* AMY *with pillows.* MISS PIGGY (AMY *dressed up*) *is revealed in an upright bed.*

MISS P. Kermy? Kermy!?

KERMIT (*Kermit puppet pops up from under the sheets*). Er... yes, Miss Piggy?

MISS P. I thought I'd use the *Sesame Street* time machine to go back in time and kill baby Hitler.

KERMIT. Did Bert and Ernie put you up to this?

MISS P. No! I can think for myself, thank you! Smash the patriarchy.

She produces a gun.

KERMIT. A gun?! Where did you...

MISS P. Fozzie Bear.

KERMIT. But Miss Piggy. If you go back in time and kill Hitler *prior* to his atrocities, won't you be removing the reason you're going back to kill him?

ACT ONE, SCENE FIVE 25

MISS P....Dohhhh!! Hi-yaaa! (*She karate chops* KERMIT.)

SFX: EastEnders *DUFF DUFF DUFF.* AMY *exits.*

DAVE. Alright, now we're cooking on gas.

MICHAEL (*to audience*). I just need to point out that travelling *back* in time is far more complicated than travelling *forwards*. Basically because –

DAVE. Exactly. Third and definitely final paradox!

MICHAEL. The Timeline Protection Paradox.

MICHAEL *turns the page on the flipchart. Underscore from the TV show* The Crown. AMY *enters as* MEGHAN MARKLE.

MEGHAN. H? H?!

MICHAEL. I give up. (*Sits.*)

DAVE *enters as* PRINCE HARRY. *Autobiography in hand.*

HARRY. What is it, Meghan?

MEGHAN. This toxic family is beyond repair. And I know just how to fix it.

HARRY. More chickens? Our own therapy game show on Netflix!

MEGHAN. No. Go back in time and kill Queen Victoria.

She produces a gun.

HARRY. M, I absolutely massively support anything you say, but you'd need a time machine.

MEGHAN. David Hasselhoff has one in his garage.

HARRY. Cripes! Well, I guess wiping us all out is what it's finally come to. Don't forget to film it on your phone!

AMY *spins on the spot. Lights and sound signify time travel.*

MEGHAN. Here I am at Windsor Castle in the Victorian era.

DAVE *appears as* QUEEN VICTORIA.

There she is – young Victoria herself.

VICTORIA. Greetings, subjects. (*Evil.*) I will beget the most dysfunctional family in all the world!! Ha, ha, ha!!!

MICHAEL (*to the audience*). I'm so, so, sorry about this.

MEGHAN. I don't think so, Queeny! (*She fires the gun.*) Why won't it work? Why won't it work!?

VICTORIA. Because the laws of our linear universe prevent foolish girls like you from ever killing or saving *anyone* retrospectively! And now you'll be stuck in this paradox vortex forever! Ha ha ha!

MEGHAN. Noooo!

SFX: EastEnders *DUFF DUFF DUFF.*

DAVE. Alright! Please give it up for Michael's paradox dramatisations!

MICHAEL. They're absolutely not mine. At all.

MICHAEL strikes the flipchart then pushes the chaise longue to SL. AMY and MICHAEL are getting into period costume and moving set into position.

DAVE. Esteemed audience members, you are now fully briefed and ready to travel with us to the Victorian parlour where my great-great-grandfather's journey began. Please bear with us a moment while we prepare the stage.

MICHAEL (*reveal*). One velveteen chaise longue!

He removes the sheet and then puts the plant stand in position.

DAVE. Thank you, Michael. For the rest of this evening you will witness the horrors that centuries from now H. G. Wells had to endure. He was forced to physically and morally wrestle with –

AMY. An aspidistra plant. (*She places the plant on the USR stand.*)

DAVE. An entirely new race of humans. And then, good people of London, and likely surrounding home counties too, you will leave this theatre with a choice – a life-changing decision. Either you will choose –

ACT ONE, SCENE SIX 27

MICHAEL. Tea and biscuits. (*He has entered with table with a tray of tea.*)

DAVE. Either you will choose to help steer humanity away from the grim future my great-great-grandfather recorded, or you will choose to be –

AMY. A free-standing door. (*She pushes the door into position.*)

DAVE. A denier, a naysayer…

MICHAEL. A Persian rug. (*He lays it out.*)

DAVE. A doubting Thomas! Thank you, guys! Are we ready? Anything missing?

AMY. Adequate rehearsal time?

MICHAEL (*remembering*). An ornate drinks trolley! (*He places the trolley.*)

DAVE. Journey with us now, one hundred and twenty-eight years into the past, to the year 1895. Action.

Scene Six – A Victorian Parlour

AMY *and* MICHAEL *take their places onstage as the convivial establishing music completes. The lights come up.*
MRS RICHARDS *enters, followed by* FILBY.

MRS RICHARDS. This way please, sir.

FILBY. Well where the blazes is he, Mrs Richards?

MRS RICHARDS. I'm really not sure, sir. Can I take your coat?

Pause. He doesn't have one. A coat is thrown to FILBY, *which he then passes to* MRS RICHARDS.

FILBY. Thank you. I presume Miss Mary Selby hasn't arrived yet?

MRS RICHARDS. No. I suspect that doorbell was her though.

They wait. Eventually the doorbell rings. MRS RICHARDS *hands the coat back to* FILBY.

Please excuse me.

She exits.

FILBY. Wells, where the devil are you?

The door opens.

MRS RICHARDS (*off*). Go right on in, madame.

MARY (*off*). Thank you, Mrs Richards.

MARY *enters.*

Hello Filby.

FILBY. Mary!

MARY. Where's Bertie?

FILBY (*while handing her the coat*). Well, Mrs Richards –

MARY. Yes? I mean no. (*She hands him back the coat.*)

FILBY. – his housekeeper, said she really wasn't sure. (*He throws the coat offstage.*)

MARY. How odd. Because he insisted I arrived promptly.

FILBY. And me too – that he insisted that to… too.

MARY. His tea's still warm.

After the line she walks to the tea tray and touches a cup.

So he can't be far.

FILBY. Typical. Still, it's what we've come to expect of him.

MARY. What's that supposed to mean?

FILBY. Nothing. Forget it.

MARY. Well if you have something to say about my fiancé.

FILBY. Very well, answer me this –

There's a loud crash backstage. Not a SFX.

ACT ONE, SCENE SIX   29

MARY. Mrs Richards?

DAVE (*off*). Carry on.

FILBY. Answer me this –

MARY. Of course I love him.

Pause. They look at each other.

FILBY. Do you love him?

MARY (*unsure but saying the line because it's all she has*). On the weekend, yes. But obviously not during the week.

FILBY. Does he ever take any time off?

DAVE (*appearing around the door whispers*). Your lines are out of sync!

FILBY. Thank you, Mrs Richards.

MARY. Yes?

DAVE. No!

MARY. I mean, what kind of suspicion?

FILBY. I have a suspicion.

MARY. Oh. And that's your evidence, is it?

DAVE (*sotto*). Just skip forward!

MARY turns to the unopened door.

MARY. How can you possibly have built a time machine, Bertie?

DAVE (*off*). Obviously not that far! Go from 'Trust me…'

MARY. Trust me, I'm his best friend.

FILBY. And I'm engaged to be his wife.

WELLS *now bursts through the door* (DAVE *dressed in period costume*).

WELLS. I've done it! I have done it! What time do you make it? Exactly.

FILBY. Seven thirty-three.

WELLS. And the date?

MARY. The 21st of June.

WELLS. Then I can confirm it! All the physics you were taught at school is false.

FILBY. For goodness' sake get a hold of yourself, man – there are women present!

WELLS. Listen to me. You've been taught that a mathematical line between two points has no real existence, correct?

FILBY. He's at it again. Strap on. In! Bloody Mary, Mary?

MARY. Chin chin.

WELLS. So, what about an instantaneous cube?

FILBY. What on this good earth are you banging on about? Lemon?

Snappy routine with cocktail interjection that irritates DAVE.

MARY. One slice. Four-dimensional theory.

WELLS. Exactly, Mary.

FILBY. Olive?

WELLS. Four-dimensional theory.

MARY. And Tabasco.

FILBY. Well yes, I knew that. I was just checking if Mary –

MARY. I have a distinction in higher maths, Filby. You didn't even turn up to the exam.

WELLS. So –

FILBY. Celery?

WELLS. Can an object – ?

MARY. Rather.

WELLS. – that has no time duration –

FILBY. Leaves on?

WELLS. – be said to exist!?

FILBY. Umbrella?

WELLS. Here, Mary! Your cocktail! So, can an object that has no time duration be said to exist?

He grabs it and delivers it.

FILBY. No of course not. Unless it's yes. Oh batter a cod, I don't care. What's your damn obsession with time?

WELLS. The blinkered way we choose to perceive it, that's what!

MARY. Well on the subject of time, Bertie, we must set a date for the wedding.

WELLS. And I promise you we will, my love, but I really must explain this first. Let us imagine for a moment that on the surface of this sheet of paper… on this sheet of paper…

He can't locate the prop about his person. He resorts to taking an audience programme (or similar).

On the surface of this programme lives a species who have only ever known motion forwards, backwards and from left to right; that's two dimensions. Now, I'm going to speak to them. 'Hello little people who live on the page, how are you?' Now where might they think I'm contacting them from?

FILBY. A lunatic asylum.

WELLS. They can hear me, Filby, they just can't see me. So therefore I must…?

FILBY. Seek immediate medical attention.

MARY. Exist.

WELLS. Thank you, Mary. But just as they cannot perceive a third dimension of space, we cannot perceive a fourth dimension of time. But does that mean we cannot travel over it, as if it were a landscape?

FILBY. Listen to him. Mad as a wet hen! You will never convince me that we can 'fly through time', Bertie.

WELLS. Oh, is that so?

WELLS *produces an ornate, intricately constructed object (a miniature time-travelling machine) and places it on a table.*

You, my friends, are about to witness a revelation in modern science. This creation is the apogee of ten years' work on the forefront of particle physics.

MARY. It's very beautiful.

WELLS. I'm glad you think so, Mary.

FILBY. An armchair for a mouse. Bravo! Time well spent.

WELLS. Now. Who wants to play God?

FILBY. Alright, this nonsense has gone far enough.

He walks towards the door then stops. WELLS *points at him.*

WELLS. Wait!

FILBY *turns back.*

Mary? Push that little lever, forwards. Go ahead.

MARY *gingerly pushes the lever. In a flash, the model disappears.*

MARY. Oh my goodness! Where did it go?

AMY *is unconvinced that the audience are impressed but* DAVE *is incredibly proud of his trick.*

WELLS. Into the future!

FILBY. The future?! Oh shut your beef cheeks!

MARY. But how could you design such a thing?

WELLS. Just in the same way that one can fall in love but never really know how or why. How you both choose to accept this is up to you but please don't pretend you're not more than a little amazed.

FILBY. I'm more than a little hungry. Mrs Richards?!

AMY. Yes? I mean no.

WELLS *grabs* FILBY *by the collar and shakes him in an over-blocked fashion.*

WELLS. Filby, you are a fool, man! Do you not understand what you've just seen?

MARY *makes a similarly over-blocked move to get between them.*

MARY. Bertie, leave him be – (*She throws herself on the chaise longue.*) Oh, leave him be!

WELLS. And what's more, upstairs I have a prototype I've been testing for human transportation.

FILBY. Right, that's it. You've lost your mind. I'm leaving. (*He opens the door.*) Mrs Richards, my coat please.

MARY. Perhaps we should both leave and allow you to calm down.

AMY *runs around the outside of the door, throws* FILBY *his coat through the door then returns to her position onstage.*

WELLS (*through door*). But Mary, we're just getting started! Please come back.

MARY (*from downstage of him*). Get some rest, my love. You look exhausted! But it really was an astonishing trick.

She follows FILBY *through the door.* WELLS *looks as though he's going to follow but takes up a dramatic pose at the door instead. Music and light.*

WELLS. A trick?! A trick?! (*Nothing is happening.*) A TRICK?!?! And lights please.

Blackout.

AMY. I said we needed more rehearsal.

DAVE. We can still be heard in the dark, Amy.

Lights up.

There we go. Thank you!

MICHAEL. Chapter Two. Wells, the time traveller, sets off on his epic journey.

Scene Seven – Wells Sets Off

Quick re-establishing music. FILBY *and* MARY *are in fixed point, waiting for the scene to begin.* WELLS *enters his living room.*

FILBY. Now look here, Bertie, even if you could time travel –

WELLS. Which I can.

FILBY. That disappearing-toy thing was just a parlour trick.

WELLS. Except it can't be.

FILBY. Except it can be.

WELLS. Can't be.

FILBY. Can be.

WELLS. Can't be.

MARY. Would you both stop with your canning and canting!

FILBY. Mary, he's about to leap into the future with no guarantee he can ever return.

WELLS. I thought you said you don't believe in it?

FILBY. I don't. I'm just thinking of Mary.

A horse neighs outside. They notice.

MARY. I can think for myself, thank you!

FILBY *spits out a drink he's mixed.*

FILBY. Damn, I've put vodka in my whisky sour! Where are my reading glasses? I must have left them on the train.

MARY. Bertie, why not live your life and simply be happy seeing how it turns out?

WELLS. Because it's not about *my* life, Mary. Or yours. Or that idiot's. This is about the lives of our descendants. The very future of humanity.

FILBY. Okay, let's suppose you *can* time travel. If you come back with depressing news, everybody's going to think 'Well what's the point of even trying?' And if it's positive news, everyone will become complacent and it'll go down the Swanee anyway.

WELLS. Alright, so by that logic, if you knew your house was going to burn down, you wouldn't make efforts to save it? Or what about something much, much, worse?

MARY. But where does it end?

FILBY. Quite. It's plain irresponsible.

WELLS. Irresponsible? Was it irresponsible to discover the earth isn't flat? Or that it revolves around the sun? *You* might be content to stand behind a closed door, Filby, but I'd rather die trying to open it.

MARY. Bertie, what if all you do is cross over into a parallel universe?

WELLS. Don't worry, darling, I'll be back in the blink of an eye. You won't even know I've gone.

FILBY. Pah! You won't fool me!

WELLS *exits. A very quick and significant whoosh and FX.*

Scene Eight – Wells Returns from the Future, One Minute into the Past

Quick re-establishing music. FILBY *and* MARY *are in fixed point (exactly as before) waiting for the scene to begin.* WELLS *enters his living room.*

FILBY. Now look here, Bertie, even if you could time travel –

WELLS. Which I can.

FILBY. That disappearing-toy thing was just a parlour trick.

WELLS. Except it can't be.

FILBY. Except it can be.

WELLS. You've no idea I've been and returned, have you?

FILBY. From where?

WELLS. From one minute into the future. I'll prove it. Mary, your secret worry is that all I'll do is cross over into a parallel universe.

MARY. Well, that's true. It is!

WELLS. And a horse is about to neigh outside.

A horse neighs outside.

And you don't have your reading glasses, do you, Filby? You left them on the train.

FILBY. How the devil…

WELLS. Because I've done it! Ha ha! And I must do it again. I have to find out where this all leads. Goodbye. Again. To the distant future, here I go.

He exits.

Scene Nine – Wells Travels Thirty-Four Years into the Future

Big sound score. The chair we recognise from the 1960s film version of The Time Machine *emerges from USC, with* WELLS *strapped in. He speeds into the future and watches history unfold before him. The soundtrack charts time passing in a mash of fast-forward SFX, including aeroplanes, twenties music, gunfire, cheering.* WELLS*'s voice-over is heard to say 'Five years into the future. Ten years. Forty years into the future!'* WELLS *sees* MARY *enter the frame. She is much older.*

WELLS. Mary…? Mary!

He hits a button and the chair powers down. We're on a street. MARY *crosses.* WELLS *steps out of the chair.*

Mary?

MARY *turns back.*

MARY. Can I help you?… Bertie?!

ACT ONE, SCENE NINE   37

WELLS. Yes.

MARY. Oh goodness. You're alive. It's been over forty years.

WELLS. And yet I've literally just left you.

MARY. You haven't changed a bit.

WELLS. Do you believe me now, Mary? You must be amazed.

MARY. I'm... overwhelmed.

SFX: an early-twentieth-century car passes and hoots. Followed by a plane.

WELLS. What the devil is that?

MARY. A motor car.

WELLS. And the machines in the sky?

MARY. Aeroplanes? They made a big difference in the war. Filby was a sergeant major.

WELLS. Filby? You and he are still friends – that's wonderful.

MARY. Friends? No, we're married.

WELLS. Married?

MARY. Thirty-three years this past July!

WELLS. No, no, I'm afraid that can't happen. (*Aside.*) No matter, I can deal with that later.

MARY. All three of our boys were decorated.

WELLS. You have sons?

MARY. Sid never returned.

WELLS. Mary, I'm so sorry. But... what about me?

MARY. You?

WELLS. Yes. Presumably I am famous as H. G. Wells, the inventor of time travel.

MARY. Well... the truth is, Bertie, you're not really known for anything. You just vanished.

WELLS (*inner realisation*). I was travelling through time but not a part of it.

MARY. So what's it like? Tell me about the wonders you've seen.

WELLS. Well, so far it's... well, it's a lot like this. I've only come this far.

MARY. So you went to all the trouble of inventing time travel just so you could go through life faster than your friends and loved ones?

WELLS. No!

SFX: an early-twentieth-century car draws up.

FILBY (*off*). Darling? Are you coming?

WELLS. Filby?

MARY. No, Bertie. (*To off.*) I'm coming! It really was wonderful to see you, Bertie. Please look after yourself.

WELLS. Mary!

MARY. No! Goodbye.

She exits.

FILBY (*off*). Are you okay, my love? Who was that chap?

MARY (*off*). Just an old friend.

SFX: the car departs. WELLS *returns to the machine.*

WELLS. What a fool I was to visit a date within my own lifespan. I shouldn't have been diverted from my goal. To the distant future, here I go. But wait... I've lost Mary to Filby... how could that happen? Because I didn't return to prevent it. Yes. I shall return to the past, I shall marry Mary and *then* explore the distant future. Wait, what's wrong with the dials? It won't let me go back more than one minute. Damn! Think, Bertie, think! Yes – surely in the future the mechanics of travelling to the past beyond more than one minute will be more fully understood. So I shall just jump forward to that point. I'll set the dial for the year 3000 AD.

He does so and pushes the lever forward. A hair-raising whoosh.

Here we go!

Scene Ten – Wells Travels Far Into the Future

AMY, *à la* Stars in their Eyes, *enters as Cher and sings 'Turn Back Time'. Smoke, LX effects – the whole shebang, supported by* DAVE *and* MICHAEL *and using the machine as a platform. They've really rehearsed this bit.* MICHAEL *upstages* AMY *by twirling ribbons on sticks. At the key change,* MICHAEL *hands* DAVE *an electric guitar for a solo.* MICHAEL *enters with a big leaf blower which blows* AMY*'s wig off. During the song,* DAVE *interjects at various points by calling out the passing of time as follows:*

WELLS (*voice-over*). One thousand years into the future!

Then:

Two thousand years!

Then:

Three thousand years. I can't stop!

At the end of the song a huge cosmic wrenching as time screeches to a halt. DAVE *is thrown out of the machine.*

Scene Eleven – Wells Arrives in the Future and Michael Gets Stabbed

DAVE *lies motionless. A fiery sun glares overhead. Vines bend in from the wings. The world looks very odd indeed. Strange birds call in the distance.* WELLS *slowly rises.*

WELLS. Who knows how many hours, perhaps days, that I've been asleep? I've woken up in a future I hardly recognise. This must be the very ground, such as it is, where my home once stood. Yet I recognise nothing. The chronometer reads... 802,700 AD?! But what of humans?

The vines rustle, we've already heard some giggling.

I could be about to find out. Who goes there? Show yourself! Come out or I'll –

WEENA *enters wearing a blue wig and sequinned flowing dress. She stares inanely into the middle distance and floats about.*

Why, hello there. Do you speak? (*To himself.*) What am I saying – even if she does speak, English will certainly be long gone. My name... is Herbert. Bertie.

WEENA. Name?

WELLS. Yes, that's me. Me.

WEENA. Mimi?

WELLS. No, no, not Mimi, I'm... alright, I am Mimi. And you are?

WEENA. Weena. Weena.

WELLS. Well... Weena... what a delight it is to meet you. Tell me, Weena, are all the people of your time as beautiful as you?

MICHAEL *tumbles onstage in a nude-suit leotard.*

Clearly not.

MICHAEL *has a knife (very similar to the one from H. G. Wells's belongings earlier). He approaches menacingly.*

MORLOCK. Mabba slava –

WEENA. A Morlock! A Morlock!

The MORLOCK *heads towards* WEENA, *about to attack.*

MORLOCK. Mabba slabba brem jacka slava –

WEENA. Mendassa roscil –

WELLS *steps in between them.*

WELLS. No! Weena, save yourself!

WEENA *exits.* WELLS *fights the* MORLOCK, *pushes him to the ground.* WELLS *heads back to his machine. The* MORLOCK *is coming back for him.*

I really must be going. If only I could get this damn time machine to work!

He slams his fist on the time machine for emphasis on that line. The machine lights up in a way that it hasn't before. There's a blinding flash and an impressive bass drop. This is hugely more impressive than the effects they've been employing so far. In fact, it feels... real! When the lights return, blocking-wise, the scene has backed up to the MORLOCK*'s entrance.* DAVE *is in the chair.*

Repeat One – MICHAEL *tumbles onstage in a nude-suit leotard.*

MORLOCK. Mabba slava.

WEENA. A Morlock! A Morlock!

The MORLOCK *heads towards* WEENA, *about to attack.*

MORLOCK. Mabba slabba brem jacka slava.

WEENA. Mendassa roscil.

Pause. AMY *looks in alarm at* DAVE, *who is still in his chair looking bemused.*

DAVE. Sorry, um... I...

WELLS *leaps out of the chair and heads towards the* MORLOCK *to save* WEENA.

WELLS. No! Weena, save yourself!

WEENA *exits.* WELLS *fights the* MORLOCK, *pushes him to the ground.* WELLS *heads back to his machine. The* MORLOCK *is coming back for him.*

I really must be going. If only I could get this damn time machine to work!

As before, he slams his fist on the time machine. It lights up and there's a blinding flash. When the lights return, blocking-wise, the scene has again backed up a few seconds.

Repeat Two – MICHAEL *tumbles onstage in a nude-suit leotard.*

MORLOCK. Mabba slava.

WEENA. A Morlock! A Morlock!

The MORLOCK *heads towards* WEENA, *about to attack.*

MORLOCK. Mabba slabba brem jacka slava.

WEENA. Mendassa roscil.

Pause. AMY *looks in alarm at* DAVE. DAVE *isn't responding. She tries to prompt him to come.*

Save me!

DAVE. Michael, Amy, why do you keep repeating this?

DAVE *is starting to panic but he steps in-between them again.*

WELLS. Oh yes... Weena, save yourself!

WEENA *exits.* WELLS *fights the* MORLOCK, *pushes him to the ground.* WELLS *heads back to his machine. The* MORLOCK *is coming back for him.*

I really must be going. If only I could get this damn time machine to work!

As before, he slams his fist on the time machine. The machine lights up and there's a blinding flash. When the lights return, for the third time, the scene has backed up a few seconds.

Repeat Three – MICHAEL *tumbles onstage in a nude-suit leotard.*

MORLOCK. Mabba slava.

DAVE. Jesus Christ, I can time travel!

WEENA. A Morlock! A Morlock!

The MORLOCK *heads towards* WEENA, *about to attack.*

MORLOCK. Mabba slabba brem jacka slava.

WEENA. Mendassa roscil.

Pause. AMY *looks in alarm at* DAVE.

Save me!

DAVE (*to audience*). Are you guys seeing this?

ACT ONE, SCENE ELEVEN 43

MORLOCK. Yah! Yah! Yah!

AMY. Michael, stop it.

> AMY *grabs* MICHAEL*'s arm and shoves the knife away from her. It goes straight into* MICHAEL*'s heart. It's instantly clear that this is serious. Very serious.* MICHAEL *collapses.* AMY *has blood on her hands.*

Oh shit. Oh shit!

DAVE. What just happened? Michael?

AMY. Dave, I don't think that was the prop knife. I felt it go in. You know like… in him.

DAVE. Oh my God.

AMY. Why wasn't it the prop knife?! He said he was going to switch it back!

DAVE. Oh, so it's Michael's fault you stabbed him?!

AMY. We need a doctor!

DAVE. Is there a doctor in the house?! Just to be clear, this is not part of the show.

AMY. What have I done?!

DAVE. I think it's pretty obvious, don't you? (*To audience.*) Could I ask you all to quickly and quietly make your way out of the theatre, there's clearly been a murder.

AMY. I didn't murder anyone.

DAVE. Well, there are quite a few witnesses, Amy.

> DAVE *looks up then starts calmly walking away toward the time machine.*

AMY. Michael??! (*She slaps him.*) Michael! (*Slaps him again.*) Michael – (*Another slap.*)

DAVE. Amy, stop slapping him. I've had an idea. There's something we should try.

AMY. Thank God. What are you thinking?

DAVE. I think I can time travel.

AMY. What?!

DAVE. I don't think this is my great-great-grandfather's lecturing chair. I think it's the machine he used to travel through time.

AMY. Are you actually insane?!?

DAVE. No. Amy, I think I can fix this. I can go back. I can switch the knives. Amy, we are going to be okay.

ASM enters with first-aid kit and runs to MICHAEL.

Um, sorry about the, unforeseen, um… well, sorry. We were due for a short interval about now anyway, so it's probably best to head to the bar and grab yourself a nice drink, I think we could probably do with one. Maybe some snacks? And we'll see you back here in twenty minutes for the conclusion of *The Time Machine*. Hopefully.

AMY. Dave! Lights please!

Blackout/curtains close.

End of Act One.

ACT TWO

Scene Twelve – Scene One Again

Pre-set: USR: a chaise longue covered with a sheet, a stand for a plant. USL: a drinks trolley covered with a sheet, a set of steps.

Music, swirling lights and smoke ('Immigrant Song' by Led Zeppelin or 'Step on Up' by Rockin' For Decades). After a few seconds the announcement begins.

DAVE (*over music*). Esteemed audience members, welcome to this wonderful theatre. Prepare to be amazed and please welcome to the stage, Dave –

The announcement and music cuts. Pause. MICHAEL *appears* (*in rehearsal-room clothes*).

MICHAEL. Please just bear with us.

Music/announcement immediately restarts.

DAVE (*over music*). Esteemed audience members, welcome to this wonderful theatre. Prepare to be amazed and please welcome to the stage, Dave –

Announcement and music cuts again. MICHAEL *enters again and straight off the back of this…*

MICHAEL. Right, well that's all gone tits up. Hello.

He has a laptop (*that runs the show*). AMY *appears* (*in rehearsal-room clothes*), *upbeat.* MICHAEL *is pressing keys.*

AMY (*bold, keeping energy up*). But no worries, hello, because sometimes a challenge can become an opportunity.

MICHAEL (*distracted*). Yes.

AMY. For a song.

MICHAEL. No!

AMY (*upbeat announcement*). So while we resolve this technical issue, London, this is 'Believe' by the global icon, Cher! (*Straight in with the first three lines of the song, sung a cappella.*)

MICHAEL *has been looking to the wings.* (*Where's* DAVE?) *He's pressing keys. 'Immigrant Song' kicks in. He switches it off.*

MICHAEL. We're sorted.

AMY (*sotto*). Where's Dave?

MICHAEL. Don't know. (*Covering.*) Tonight you're going to bear witness to a revelation about H. G. Wells's writing that will change the way you view the world. For ever.

AMY. That's right! And we're just waiting for our third cast member to join us.

MICHAEL. Now, I appreciate that most of you have come here tonight expecting to be entertained. You need to let that thought go.

AMY. You really do.

MICHAEL. Who are we?! My name is Michael O'Reilly – actor AND company tour booker. And this is…

AMY. Amy Tymes – actor and singer.

MICHAEL. That's right.

AMY. And right now, about to join us, is Dave Wells.

MICHAEL. Just actor. Dave… Wells?! A coincidence?

AMY. No.

AMY *and* MICHAEL. Because he is –

You go.

Because he is –

I'll go.

Because he is –

ACT TWO, SCENE TWELVE   47

AMY. – actually the great-great-grandson of Herbert George Wells himself.

DAVE *enters through the audience and jumps onstage, much to* MICHAEL *and* AMY*'s surprise.*

DAVE. Hello again. Right, here we go.

AMY. Finally!

MICHAEL. And what Dave's about to tell you, he doesn't expect you to fully comprehend at once, do you.

DAVE. Yeah, yeah, yeah, forget that, you need to listen to me.

MICHAEL. We certainly didn't.

AMY. Nope. Seemed like total bullsh...

DAVE. Amy, Michael. Stop! You're both experiencing a reality where we've just begun the show. Yes? One in which we *haven't* already performed the first half tonight? Whereas I've repeated it, I don't know how many times, and every time it ends the same – with Michael's death.

During his next dialogue, DAVE *is pushing the chaise longue downstage and pulling off the covering sheet. There is a board on the chaise longue.*

Now, I appreciate it might look like I've completely lost my mind but I'll soon prove to you that I haven't. As I said, I've repeated this scenario countless times and at this exact moment Michael always says –

MICHAEL. Right, I'm leaving the stage.

DAVE *shows the board. In large lettering it reads: 'Right, I'm leaving the stage.'*

DAVE. Michael?

MICHAEL *is in shock.* DAVE *heads USC.*

AMY. Okay, I don't know why you're both doing this but can I just say, it's not funny. I'm very sorry, everyone, I really have no idea what's going on.

DAVE *pulls the free-standing door onstage. A large piece of cloth, attached to the door, in large lettering reads: 'Okay, I don't know why you're both doing this but can I just say, it's not funny. I'm very sorry, everyone, I really have no idea what's going on.'*

DAVE (*drawing her attention to the lettering*). Amy?

AMY. Oh God.

DAVE. And in – (*Checks his watch.*) five seconds' time, a few pieces of confetti will drop from the flies. Three, two, one –

Some confetti falls from the flies, as earlier.

MICHAEL. Why… have you set all this up?

DAVE *heads to the drinks trolley. He positions it further downstage and removes the cloth covering it.*

DAVE. Michael, I haven't. I've discovered time travel. Well, more stumbled on it really. It was under our noses the whole time! My great-great-grandfather's 'lecturing chair' –

AMY (*re: audience*). Are *they* all in on this?

DAVE. Amy?

He shows the back of a tray from the drinks trolley that reads: 'No they're not.'

I've been trying to save you, Michael. But every time I try, the outcome is always the same. The Timeline Protection Paradox we discuss in scene five? Yeah? Well it's all true. Now watch that LED light –

FX: the light blows.

Badly patched. How would I know that? Because you've already told me.

MICHAEL. But it's been PAT tested.

DAVE. Are you starting to believe?

AMY. No. And cards on the table, Dave – I never actually believed your great-great-grandfather time travelled! No one does!

ACT TWO, SCENE TWELVE 49

MICHAEL. She's right. In this show we just come across as three idiots trying to be clever.

DAVE. Such betrayal!

He opens his shirt, his T-shirt beneath reads: 'Betrayal.'

But obviously not news to me any more.

AMY. Dave, you're scaring me. Have you taken something?

DAVE *turns. The back of his T-shirt reads: 'I'm not on drugs.'*

DAVE. People of Finsbury and boroughs beyond, I need you to forget that you're a theatre audience. Please ignore your ability to suspend your disbelief. And instead, fully engage your rationality. Why? Because this shit just got real.

MICHAEL. Dave, this show has a family rating.

DAVE. Trust me, that's the least of your worries now, mate.

AMY. Right, since for some unknown reason you're insisting on ruining our play, here's how your stupid game doesn't quite work – (*To audience member.*) Madam, hi, could you please tell me the time?

AUDIENCE 1. Eight-fifty. (*Or whatever the actual time is.*)

AMY. What? No, We've just started the show, it must be just after seven-thirty, your watch is wrong. (*She tries elsewhere.*) You, what time is it?

AUDIENCE 2. Eight-fifty.

MICHAEL. Wait… what?

This information has surprised DAVE *as well.*

DAVE. Wow, fascinating. This has never actually happened before. Everyone, please raise your hand if you think it's roughly eight-fifty?

Everyone does.

Amazing. So this can only mean one thing –

MICHAEL. That you've somehow coerced this whole audience?

DAVE. If you've been coerced by me, please leave your hand raised. Or better still raise the other one. Or better yet raise both hands!

No one does.

See. No coercion.

AMY. Clear *proof* of it, if you ask me.

DAVE. This is absolutely fascinating. (*He picks someone else at random.*) Madam, have you already seen the first half of this play tonight?

AMY. She's gonna lie and say yes, isn't she?!

DAVE. Let her speak. Have you?

AUDIENCE 3. Yes.

AMY. Well done! Great acting, lady.

DAVE (*to audience member*). Ignore her. Please stay focused on me. So you know what happens to Michael at the end of the first half?

AUDIENCE 3. Yes.

DAVE. Brilliant. Please describe what you saw. In as much detail as you like.

AUDIENCE 3 (*words to the effect of*). Amy stabs Michael.

AMY. I stab him?!

DAVE. Michael, you were holding the wrong knife. You made a mistake in setting the props. Go and check.

MICHAEL *exits.*

AMY. Okay listen here, lady. I'm quite a volatile person and I don't react well to this kind of thing. Swear on your life that you saw me stab Michael.

AUDIENCE 3. I swear on my life.

AMY. May that heinous lie rest on your conscience for ever!

DAVE. Finsbury Parkers, please raise your right hand for me. There are two actors on this stage. Please point to the one you believe to be the killer.

ACT TWO, SCENE TWELVE 51

Everyone points at AMY. MICHAEL *returns from wings with the real knife. He tests the blade.*

MICHAEL. It's true. I've set the wrong knife. It shouldn't have been this one.

He gives it to DAVE, *fetches the box and takes the fake one out of it.* AMY *is hyperventilating.*

DAVE. Amy, you need to get a grip. Michael dies onstage. And I don't mean like when he tried stand-up.

MICHAEL. Hey.

AMY. Wait. So if what you're saying is true – and it's clearly not – why do we just keep repeating the same thing? What's the point?

DAVE. I don't know. I think there's probably no point. Every time I go back I'm just desperately hoping that *something* will change the outcome. Are you okay, Michael?

MICHAEL. No! Obviously not!

DAVE. Amy?

AMY. This is *literally* an actor's panic dream.

DAVE *checks his watch and points at the* USHER.

DAVE. The usher's phone is about to ring.

SFX: phone rings.

It's the vet. Don't worry, Madam Floofkina is going to be fine.

The USHER *exits hurriedly, answering the phone.*

(*To* AMY.) It's her dog.

AMY. Stop with the predictions! And who has a dog called Madam Floofkina? Okay so... and I can't believe I'm asking this... *how* are you time travelling?

DAVE. Using my great-great-grandfather's machine.

AMY. You're telling me that ridiculous chair thing can transport you through time?

DAVE. It did for him and it has for me. As you're about to further witness.

MICHAEL. Right, I'm going to tell you something now that I've never told anyone in my life.

DAVE (*to* AMY). This is pretty candid.

MICHAEL. So, if you're telling the truth you'll know what it is, because you'll have already witnessed me saying it, right?

DAVE. Yeah. And I wasn't going to make a big deal out of it, but...

DAVE wheels out a big display board with a sheet over it.

Derren Brown – eat your heart out! Go ahead, Michael.

AMY. You don't have to do this, Michael.

Dramatic pause.

MICHAEL. When I was thirteen, I punched a swan.

DAVE. And our survey says...!

SFX: game-show winning sting. DAVE removes the sheet from the board and in flashing lights, it...

Reads...

Swan puncher!

MICHAEL. I really don't like this!

AMY. And what happens now? Cos obviously we can't continue with the rest of the show.

DAVE. Well, the next thirty-five minutes always plays out slightly differently. Once you sang every song from Cher's back catalogue and this whole audience stood up... and left. Apart from this guy – (*Points at audience member.*) He loved it. But as I say, the outcome is always the same.

AMY. So you're telling me we're all just waiting here for Michael to die?

DAVE. I wouldn't have put it so insensitively, but yes. Correct. Michael, make yourself useful. Go and get my chair.

Scene Thirteen – Michael Tries to Leave

DAVE. London, I'm sure you have some burning questions, so please do fire away. And don't worry – no question is too stupid.

AMY. If it's 'Can I get a refund on my ticket?' then yes, obviously you can.

DAVE. No, absolutely not! Why?

AMY. Why?! Because they've booked to see a production of *The Time Machine* and they're getting this shit.

DAVE. Family show, Amy.

AMY. I don't care, Dave!

DAVE. You forget – they've already seen the first half. Which was actually going rather well until you took out a cast member.

MICHAEL. This is really doing my head in.

DAVE. And in all honesty, I'm hoping that I can convince you both to perform an abridged version of the second act before Michael dies.

MICHAEL. Well you can forget about that, buddy.

DAVE. Trust me, I've convinced you to do a lot more than that before.

MICHAEL. What? Like what?

DAVE. Well you know that thing you can do with your penis…?

AMY. Hang on, hang on. HANG THE EFF ON! What time did, does – whatever, Michael die? End of the first half? So, about eight-thirty, right? What time is it now, sir?

AUDIENCE. Nine.

AMY. There. So the allotted time has already passed!

DAVE. In their timeline, maybe. But not in ours!

AMY. So you're trying to tell me that we three actors onstage are experiencing a completely different time dimension to the rest of the audience?

DAVE. Isn't that usually what happens in theatre? I don't know why! I'm not a scientist! Does anyone here have an explanation? In fact are there any quantum physicists in? Never asked that before.

MICHAEL. The Twin Hypothesis.

DAVE. Huh?

MICHAEL. The Twin Hypothesis explains it.

DAVE. Go for it.

MICHAEL. One twin jets off in a rocket travelling close to the speed of light –

AMY. Oh, I don't care! I don't want to know! I just need a drink.

She starts helping herself to the drinks trolley.

MICHAEL. Right, I've had enough of this. I'm leaving.

He starts to exit through the audience.

DAVE (*to the audience*). So what's happening now is Michael's brain is operating in two concurrent states. Part of him simply won't accept what's going on – 'It's absurd it's insane. There is no way this could be happening.' But the other half is telling him: 'Well if this is it, you might as well go out with a bang.' Literally.

MICHAEL *returns*.

MICHAEL. Amy, do you want to come?

AMY. What?

MICHAEL. Back to the hotel maybe.

DAVE (*to audience*). This gets very awkward.

AMY. Are you asking me to have end-of-the-world sex with you, Michael?

MICHAEL. No! (*Beat.*) Maybe. Do you want to?

AMY. Michael –

MICHAEL. Right, that's it, I quit! Goodbye!

AMY. Michael!

ACT TWO, SCENE THIRTEEN 55

MICHAEL. No. I'm not putting up with any more of this.

He exits – through the auditorium.

AMY. Michael!!

DAVE. Don't worry, he doesn't get far. (*To audience.*) So, as I mentioned, the rules that govern causality won't allow him to escape – as you all will recall from the Timeline Protection Paradox? Would you care to remind us of it, sir? Or weren't you concentrating? Meghan Markle had a gun and she couldn't kill…? Queen Victoria, that's right – Now the paradox states that a person cannot go back in time to save or destroy another person's existence. So, what happens to Michael is this – he *thinks* he's going into the bar next door. When in actual fact at that exact moment he'll come in through this door here – (*Centre-stage.*) He'll say: 'What the hell? What's going on?' And then call me a bastard and then throw himself dramatically on the chaise longue and cry for a bit and then he'll say: 'Why me, why me?' Like, a lot. Everyone count with me… he's coming in, in… five, four, three, two and one…

MICHAEL *bursts onto the stage through the free-standing door.*

MICHAEL (*looks in disbelief*). What the hell? What's going on?! (*He starts to well up.*) You bastard.

He approaches DAVE *and makes a pathetic attempt to hit him.*

Why me? Why me? Why? Why me? Why… me?

AMY. Michael, listen to me! I'm not going to kill you.

DAVE. Although two hundred witnesses say you already have. Not intentionally of course, I mean they're all accidents. But whatever happens – (*Checks watch.*) in thirty minutes' time…

MICHAEL. What do you mean 'they're *all* accidents'?

DAVE. Well once you were electrocuted – not strictly Amy's fault but you shouldn't have left that bare wire in the wings. A panic-induced heart attack.

MICHAEL. I'm thirty-two!

DAVE. Self-injected bleach.

MICHAEL. Bleach?!

AMY. So hang on! You're telling me they're not all my fault?

DAVE. No, no, no. Only the first time. Completely random after that.

AMY. Well you could have flipping told me that! I've been sitting here feeling really guilty!

DAVE. You swallowed a wasp.

AMY. Not my fault either.

DAVE. You let it out of a jar.

AMY. Damn!

MICHAEL (*sarcastic*). Run over by a clown car?!

DAVE. It'll be in there somewhere.

MICHAEL. Right, I'm making some calls.

DAVE (*to audience*). Starting with his mum.

MICHAEL. How have you got my phone?

DAVE *hands* MICHAEL, MICHAEL's *phone*.

DAVE. Which doesn't end well – as you'll see. But you'd do the same, wouldn't you. If it was you.

DAVE *makes himself a cocktail*.

MICHAEL (*on phone*). Mum? Fine. No, not fine. It's just that I might not be able to speak to you again... because Dave says he can time travel and... no, no, please listen... yes I do realise you're at work...

AMY. Isn't she a doctor?

DAVE. Cardiologist.

MICHAEL. No, this isn't more of my acting nonsense. Dave says he can predict the future and... Mum? Mum!? Mum!! Damn.

ACT TWO, SCENE THIRTEEN 57

MICHAEL *makes another call.*

DAVE. In fairness, she's a busy woman.

AMY. Michael, let's just take a moment, shall we?

DAVE *spins round the board onstage. On the other side it reads: 'Michael summons all three emergency services, ambulance, police, fire.'*

MICHAEL (*on the phone*). I'm not sure – police probably. And an ambulance, definitely. Maybe the fire service too? Yes, a fatality. Me. In…

DAVE *holds up a card that reads: 'Twenty-seven minutes, mate.'*

Twenty-seven minutes, mate. I mean twenty-seven minutes. No, I'm not on any kind of medication. Yes there *are* people with me. Including the perpetrator.

AMY *is having a realisation.*

(*Into phone.*) Well in a court of law it'd probably be manslaughter. Yes, I'll hold.

AMY (*revelation*). Oh my God!

DAVE (*re:* AMY). And here we go: revelation number one.

AMY. Okay, very funny. I'm so stupid! I'm SO stupid! Where are the cameras? This is some kind of *Candid Camera* set-up thing, isn't it? Is the Park Theatre in on this? Why would you set all of this up to completely humiliate me?! It's because you're scared of strong powerful women, isn't it?!

DAVE. That's not true.

MICHAEL. That is true, actually. (*And then back to phone.*) Hello?

DAVE. Amy, there are clearly no cameras here. And answer me this – when have you ever seen Michael be this convincing at acting?

MICHAEL. How dare you! I actually resent that!

DAVE. See. Have you ever seen him be that credible with a scripted line? Ever? Be honest – *have you*?

AMY. No.

MICHAEL. Oh, well thanks very much, guys! (*Into phone.*) Hello? I'm dying!

DAVE. And cue revelation number two...

AMY. Right. Where's your great-great-grandfather's machine?

DAVE. Backstage. All set up for you.

AMY. What do you mean, 'all set up'?

DAVE. Well you want to try it out for yourself, don't you. (*To the audience.*) You know, it never fails to amaze me how long it takes her to have this idea.

AMY (*very sarcastic*). Yes please, Dave. I really, really want to try out this machine. Because I really, really believe it might be true. Cos I'm just *such* an impossibly stupid and gullible woman!

DAVE. You're not. Just go and sit in the machine.

AMY (*more sarcastic*). Okay, Dave, I'll just go over to stage-left...

DAVE. That's stage-right.

AMY. Don't patronise me!

She exits SR.

DAVE. Michael, your phone's about to run out of juice.

MICHAEL (*at phone*). No, no. Damn.

AMY (*from wings, even more sarcastic/unbelieving*). Oh look at this – a time-travelling machine! Wow, I wonder how it works?

DAVE. Just push the red button and pull the lever at the same time.

AMY (*as sarcastic as it's possible to be*). I'm so excited! I'm going to travel into the future. Well here I go. You twonk!

SFX: the stage effects of ACTUAL time travel again.

Scene Fourteen – Amy Believes

DAVE. Michael, watch out.

The free-standing door swings opens and MICHAEL *is hit in the face.*

AMY. Shit the bed, you've got to be kidding me!

DAVE. I know.

AMY. It's a shitting time machine!

DAVE. Family show. I know!

AMY. It's amazing! It's incredible!

DAVE. We got there in the end.

AMY. It's just terrible. It's terrible what happens to Michael.

DAVE. Terrible. Every time.

AMY. Like... *every* time. It makes you ask really big questions about the universe!

DAVE. Well it certainly puts the old 'Determination versus Free Will' debate to bed.

AMY. I mean, he just can't avoid it.

DAVE. Nope.

AMY. The first few times it was profoundly upsetting. But like by the twentieth time, it became strangely engrossing.

MICHAEL. Hey!

AMY. And sometimes it's... well, funny. I don't mean funny-ha-ha-funny. I mean... like, when you choked on a balloon animal.

DAVE. No?! How is that even possible?

MICHAEL. Guys, please!

AMY. Or when he suffocates, dressed as a dinosaur?

DAVE. Where on earth did a dinosaur costume come from?

AMY. That prop cupboard.

MICHAEL. Guys!

DAVE. Michael, please, I'm trying to have a conversation with Amy. I saw one where he had a sneezing attack and headbutted the pros arch. (*Or equivalent alternative.*)

AMY. I had that! Strangled by a curtain?

DAVE. Yep.

AMY. Fatal backwards-somersault attempt?

DAVE. Ouch.

AMY. That guy in three-C chucks a tin of beans at his head?

MICHAEL (*to audience*). Oh cheers, mate!

DAVE. Who brings a tin of beans to the theatre?

AMY. And he was pecked to death by that swan.

DAVE. Revenge attack. Nice! So how many did you watch?

AMY. Hundreds! There's literally an infinite number of possibilities.

MICHAEL. For Christ's sake!

AMY. Michael, listen we're not laughing *at* you.

DAVE. No! Or even really *with* you.

AMY. We're just fundamentally...

DAVE. Devastated.

AMY. Yeah that's all it is. Tragic. And bizarre.

DAVE. Shocking.

AMY. Meaningless. And amazing – the spontaneous combustion?

DAVE. No!

MICHAEL. Right, that's it...

   MICHAEL *heads for the wings*.

AMY. Michael, Michael, Michael. The machine won't work for you.

DAVE. Believe me, I really thought that was a solution.

AMY. We both did.

DAVE. It seems the universe prevents it.

MICHAEL (*offstage*). Work! Work! You damn thing.

DAVE. Space–time continuum, mate.

MICHAEL (*offstage*). Somebody… please help me!

DAVE. We've tried. Nobody can.

Scene Fifteen – The University Plan – Amy Has a Brainwave

AMY. Hang on, hang on, hang on!

DAVE. What?

AMY. Nobody *existing* can. Because nobody existing has figured out the space–time continuum. But –

DAVE. This is a new idea, right?

AMY. Yes, I've tried loads of others already, but this… this could actually work! Give me a moment…

DAVE. Interesting. Uncharted waters once again. (*To audience.*) From the outside this must be fascinating. But I must reassure you, if this is your first trip to the theatre please don't be put off.

MICHAEL *enters through the door with a gun to his head.*

MICHAEL. I don't see any point in stringing this out!

DAVE. – It's not normally like this.

MICHAEL. Goodbye, everyone.

DAVE. Will you grow up, Michael, Amy's trying to think. And that is a prop gun.

MICHAEL *pulls the trigger and a bang flag drops down from the barrel.*

AMY. We need to contact the future. Bear with me on this. Does anyone here have a close connection to a university?

DAVE. I've no idea what she's doing? Michael?

MICHAEL. I was actually having quite a happy life.

AMY. Someone, please. Or has anyone been to university?

If someone has their hand raised.

Which one?

Whatever they say, the whole cast look downbeat.

Doesn't matter. What's your connection with – (*Name of university they've given*)?

AUDIENCE (*whatever they come back with*).

AMY. Great, thank you.

[*NB: If no one has a connection to a university, use the following fallback.*

Okay, please raise your hand if you know where University College London is.

Then choose someone with their hand raised.]

Thank you, madam. Dave, get a pen and paper. Now!

DAVE. Absolutely, you're the boss.

AMY. I'm not the boss.

DAVE. No, sure. I am.

MICHAEL. No one is!

AMY. What's your name please?

AUDIENCE. Sandra. (*Or whatever their name is.*)

DAVE *returns*.

AMY. Can you give Sandra the pen and paper?

DAVE. Okay. Not sure why. Just embracing the unknown.

AMY. Sandra's going to write a letter to the future world of science – when controlling predestination will be

ACT TWO, SCENE FIFTEEN 63

understood. She's going to explain Michael's predicament and ask them to send a solution back in time within the next twenty-three minutes.

DAVE. Amy, are you saying we get some science people from the future to tell us how to save Michael?

MICHAEL. That's actually a pretty neat idea, Dave.

DAVE. Thanks, mate.

AMY. Excuse me, that's *my* idea.

DAVE. I think we arrived at it at the same time.

AMY. Bloody men!

DAVE. Family show.

MICHAEL. Feels more like a pre-emptive wake.

DAVE. Right, how do we receive the solution from the future, Amy?

AMY. We need a phone and I don't have mine.

DAVE. Mine's on ten per cent and Michael's is dead. (*To audience member.*) Right who's got a phone? Please raise your hand if you would like to donate your phone to help us save Michael's life. Anyone? (*Does a sleight-of-hand action, so only a dummy prop phone is actually secured.*) Thank you. What's your name? Sam? Round of applause for Sam. Hang on, Sam, what network are you with?

AMY. What?

DAVE. Just in case that presents a problem.

AMY. If scientists in the distant future have cracked sending messages back in time, I hardly think they're going to be stumped by a twenty-first-century phone network.

DAVE. Be a shame if that were a stumbling block.

AMY. Fine! Who are you with, Sam?

SAM. EE. (*Or whatever.*)

The whole cast look downbeat at whatever the network is.

DAVE. It'll have to do. Make a note of that, Sandra. Sam, please call out your number so Sandra can write it down. Now, Sam!

SAM (DAVE *and* AMY *play with whatever comes*). Zero-seven-nine-seven-zero-three-four-five-one-two-seven.

MICHAEL. If you're lying it's my blood on your hands!

DAVE *sets up a plinth for the phone with a special (light) trained on it.*

AMY. Sandra, I need you to do two more things for me – and it's vital you follow these instructions to the letter. Firstly, I need you to take that letter you're composing, secure it in a time capsule and ensure it remains in the trust of Manchester University. But you don't have to go right now – there's no real urgency as I see it.

MICHAEL. No real urgency?

DAVE. Given the freakishness of space–time, as long as she actually does it, it doesn't matter if it's today or tomorrow. Am I right?

MICHAEL. Well yes, I suppose that's true.

DAVE (*again taking credit for* AMY*'s idea*). Yes! Get in!

MICHAEL. That particular time-based paradox centres around a dictum that states –

DAVE. Come on, Michael, read the room, buddy. No one's interested.

AMY (*back to* SANDRA). Now, to the second part of your mission, Sandra, should you choose to accept it –

DAVE. She's in way too deep to back out now. Michael's life is solely in your hands, Sandra.

AMY. Dave?

DAVE. Yes.

AMY. Shut up!

DAVE. Fair.

ACT TWO, SCENE FIFTEEN 65

AMY. A challenge such as this will require a massive funding incentive. So tomorrow, I need you to open up a savings account in the university's name, into which you'll deposit the full sum of money we're about to raise from this audience.

MICHAEL. Amy, I hardly think a bit of loose change will suffice.

AMY. Relax, Michael – you're overlooking a major factor: compound interest. Centuries' worth. Whatever we're about to raise in this room will one day amount to a huge pot that can be drawn upon to fund your survival.

DAVE. Love it. Let's start with you, Michael. Empty your pockets.

MICHAEL. I don't even...

DAVE *finds a jar.* MICHAEL *hands over change from his pocket.*

DAVE. Four pounds fifty? Well it's a start I suppose.

AMY. I've only got fifty pee.

DAVE. And we're up to a fiver. I'm all about the card these days. I don't have cash.

AMY. Dave!

DAVE. Okay, but I've only got a twenty.

AMY. Stick it in.

DAVE. Can we do change?

AMY. No!

MICHAEL. Do you believe in Amy's idea or not?

DAVE. Of course. And I've just realised that as soon as we get that call through we can take the money back anyway.

MICHAEL. No, no, no, that can't happen! If the money gets withdrawn after I survive, it will mean that the money never accumulated, and therefore there's no funding for the challenge and so the call from the future never gets made.

AMY. But what if we've already received it?

MICHAEL. Impossible. The present knows what happens in the future.

AMY. What?

MICHAEL. It's a universal law that our brains won't let us compute.

AMY. Michael. Stop. You're hurting my head!

DAVE. Right, twenty-five quid. Anyone else? Who else would like to donate to Michael's survival fund? Last chance? None of you care about Michael? No one? (*To* MICHAEL.) It's because you punched a swan. Okay, twenty-five pounds – (*Or whatever's been raised.*) it is.

AMY *hands the jar to* SANDRA.

AMY. Sandra. Please don't mess this up.

DAVE. Have you written out the challenge?

MICHAEL. Don't worry. I've done it.

He hands SANDRA *the letter and stays with her to explain her task.*

DAVE. Excellent. We'd really like to avoid another gruesome outcome tonight, please.

AMY. We must trust in the future. And if we've learned anything this evening, it's that anything is possible.

DAVE. Amy, do you think this is going to work?

AMY. Yeah, of course I do. And what's the most important thing this evening?

DAVE. My play?

AMY. It's Michael!

DAVE. Yes.

AMY. We now just need to keep him occupied until the call comes in.

MICHAEL *returns to the stage and the chaise longue.*

Michael...

MICHAEL. I always thought I'd adopt a rescue dog and live in the country.

AMY. That's gonna happen, buddy. And if for some reason it doesn't, well at least you'll have a research foundation in your name.

DAVE. Although logically, only if you survive.

AMY. Leave it, Dave!

Scene Sixteen – Michael Gets a Date and They Decide to Carry On with the Play

MICHAEL. So what happens now? Do we just have to wait for a call from someone in the future who can tell us how to break the universal time protection code?

AMY. I think so.

MICHAEL. On Sam's iPhone 3?

DAVE. It's a good phone. (*He drops it.*) Best on the market.

MICHAEL. This is madness.

Pause.

AMY. I have a suggestion.

DAVE. Right, out of interest, Amy – and I'm trying really hard not to sound sarcastic here – what possible Cher song would be appropriate in the current circumstances?

AMY. 'Save Up All Your Tears'.

DAVE. That's actually pretty good.

MICHAEL. 'Baby Don't Go'.

DAVE. Also good. 'The Shoop Shoop Song'?

AMY. No.

MICHAEL. You fool.

AMY. But I wasn't going to suggest singing a song, actually, Dave. I was going to say this is Michael's night and he should decide what happens from now on.

DAVE. That is a *good* idea, but I have a *GREAT* one. I can't help but feel that this audience would be incredibly rewarded by seeing the second half of my play.

AMY. Trust me, they wouldn't.

DAVE. So let's go from the scene where Wells sets light to the forest because the Morlocks have stolen his time machine.

AMY. No! No way. From now on it's about Michael.

DAVE. Okay, well, he's definitely heavily involved in the bit where I, I mean Wells, spends all day contemplating the earth's journey towards the sun?

AMY. Oh my God I really wish it was you I'd stabbed! Can you get it into your head, we're not doing your stupid play.

MICHAEL *starts crying*.

DAVE. For God's sake, Michael, what is it now?

AMY. He's understandably emotional, Dave! Michael, this is *your* night. The stage is yours – to do anything you like. We'll fully support *any* proposal.

Pause.

MICHAEL. I've got my poems about the ULEZ zone.

AMY. Except those, eh?

MICHAEL. That thing I can do with my pe–

DAVE. Be serious!

MICHAEL. *The Importance of Being Earnest* hip-hop dance mash-up.

AMY *and* DAVE. No!

AMY. How about something that seems like a crazy mad idea on the surface, but in reality, might not be.

MICHAEL. How do you mean? Like what?

AMY. Like, I don't know... like – (*From nowhere.*) a date with an audience member.

DAVE. What?

AMY. Come on – we can set up a table, light some candles, sort out a Deliveroo.

DAVE. Hold on. We abandon my groundbreaking play so Michael can chat up a punter over a takeaway?!

MICHAEL. I'd be up for that.

AMY. See.

DAVE. We're not doing that.

AMY. It's Michael's night.

DAVE. I don't care. We're not doing it.

AMY. Yes we are! Go and set up a table. Is there an usher in here anywhere? (*To an* USHER.) Excuse me, can we organise a bottle of red from the bar please?

MICHAEL. I'd prefer white.

AMY. White, please.

MICHAEL. Champagne actually.

DAVE. Champagne? Who the hell's paying for this?

AMY. You are.

DAVE. A bottle of white. House.

AMY. What kind of food, Michael? Go mad! Anything.

MICHAEL. I've become quite partial to Armenian cuisine.

DAVE. Get real, Michael. (*To audience.*) They do really good pizza here. Can someone order some?

AMY. Dave... music...

DAVE *chooses a track on the laptop. We get soft jazz.* AMY *takes* MICHAEL*'s hand.*

So. Who do you like the look of?

MICHAEL. Everyone looks so lovely. Let's go over this way. No. Let's try the other side. No, they're looking at the ground too. Back over here. I think I've seen someone I'd like to ask. (*Someone is chosen.*)

AMY. Thank you. Round of applause for…?

AUDIENCE. Jordan.

AMY. For Jordan please.

> JORDAN *is brought onstage and takes a seat at the table with* MICHAEL *as a bottle of wine arrives. The* USHER *presents the bill to a reluctant* DAVE.

(*To* DAVE.) Dave! Credit card, please.

DAVE. Can't we just use the money in the jar?

AMY. Credit card!

DAVE. Fine.

> *He concedes and does the transaction with the* USHER*'s mobile device.* AMY *has located a camera.*

MICHAEL (*to* JORDAN). Would you like a breadstick? They are real.

AMY. Let's get a nice photo. Actually… do you know what would make this night even more memorable… Dave, go and find some paints.

DAVE. Paints?!

AMY. Now! Right, is there a professional portrait painter in the audience tonight? Okay, anyone who's ever done an art exam? An evening class? Graffiti? Anyone ever picked up a pencil? Great, sir. Round of applause for…

AUDIENCE. Laurel.

AMY. For Laurel please.

> DAVE *enters with an easel, a stool and some paints.*

(*To* LAUREL, *gesturing to* MICHAEL *and his date.*) All you have to do is paint this scene here. Now take your time, there's absolutely no pressure.

DAVE. Well... eighteen minutes to produce something both deeply respectful and memorable.

AMY. Don't worry, no one will judge you! Or laugh at your efforts. How's the date going, Jordan? Are you sensing a bit of chemistry or do you wish you'd swiped left?

JORDAN. No, he seems nice. (*Or whatever the response.*)

AMY. Michael?

MICHAEL. I'm just scared of dying.

AMY. I'll also take that as a general thumbs up. Come on, phone! Ring, you bastarding thing.

DAVE. Right, that's it. Clearly we can't present the second half of the show quite in the way we've rehearsed it. But for all you fans of H. G. Wells –

AMY. Dave, what are you doing?

DAVE. Sorting out some entertainment for their date.

AMY. Dave –

DAVE. Who would like to play that creature from the future we saw earlier? A terrifying Morlock?

AMY. No, no, no. How's that gonna work?

DAVE. Well it'll be more entertaining, and certainly a lot less awkward than watching... THIS!

MICHAEL *is feeding breadsticks to* JORDAN. (MICHAEL *can have set them up to be obliging with this.*)

Scene Seventeen – An Audience Member Takes on Michael's Role

DAVE (*to the audience*). Right, who's it going to be? Who wants to play a Morlock? You remember, the wig and the costume attacking Weena? You'll get to do a scene with me. You'll also get a costume and a script. Thank you, sir. Round of applause for...

AUDIENCE. Alan.

DAVE. For Alan! Now Alan, come on up – Alan, there's absolutely no pressure but you've basically volunteered to help me save this show. Amy is going to take you backstage and give you a script.

AMY. No I'm not.

DAVE. Yes you are. Now before we do this, Alan, I have to ask you a very serious question. How comfortable are you with improvised combat?

A lot of pizzas arrive.

Oh wow, that's a lot of pizzas! Thank you to whoever ordered them. That's extremely generous. Amy, don't leave Alan standing there.

AMY *reluctantly takes the audience member backstage.*
DAVE *dumps pizzas on the table*

DAVE. There you go, guys – fill your boots. And Jordan, feel free to spin your chair round and watch. Ah, sorry if that messes up your angles, Laurel. Although by the look of it, I assume you're going to start again anyway? So, let's recap. Wells has travelled over eight hundred thousand years into the future where he has met a strange and beautiful creature called Weena. (*Calling to* AMY.) Weena?

AMY (*off*). I'm not doing the voice.

DAVE. Do the voice.

AMY (*off*). No.

DAVE. Please?

WEENA *does her screeching.*

ACT TWO, SCENE SEVENTEEN

There she is. Now, we rejoin Wells when the Morlocks have impounded his time machine and brought him to their underground lair where he is to face judgement before the head honcho called... Well, let's just call him Alan. And you, people of Finsbury Park, will be playing the savage, brutal Morlock jury, baying for my blood. Amy, are we ready?

AMY (*off*). Yes.

DAVE. People of Finsbury Park, are you ready? I said, are you ready?! Then put your hands together for your leader – Alan, the Morlock King!

AMY *brings in* ALAN (*costumed up and with a script*) *and sits him on a throne. Dramatic music and swirling lights focus on him.* MICHAEL *encourages the audience to chant 'Alan, Alan', etc.* ALAN, *reading from a script, has a microphone with a voice effect which makes his voice sound very deep/or high.* WELLS *kneels before him.*

WELLS. What do you want with me?

ALAN. Mabba slava.

WELLS (*points at* AMY). And Weena's line!

AMY *is fixing herself a drink but half-heartedly screams.*

Don't worry, Weena, I'll save you. Admit it, Alan, the instinct for cannibalism has returned, hasn't it?

ALAN. Mabba slava.

WELLS. You wish to eat me? You're insane!

ALAN. Yummy, yummy, in my tummy!

WELLS. Well you've gone too far! Come, Weena, escape with me.

AMY *is uninterested in playing along.*

Well, if you wish to devour me, Morlock, you'll have to catch me first.

WELLS *starts running, trying to tempt* ALAN *to chase him.* MICHAEL *encourages* ALAN *then leads the audience in chanting 'Eat him, eat him...'* WELLS *throws himself to the floor, imagining being pinned to the ground, wrestling until...*

AMY. Wait, stop, stop!

Audience member SAM's phone is ringing! A call from the future? DAVE answers the phone.

DAVE. Hello... yes... Oh my goodness, really? No way! Sam, apparently you can upgrade to an iPhone 13 for only thirty pounds a month.

AMY. Oh, hang up!

DAVE. Sorry, it's not a good time. Call back. No, don't call back! Ever!

He hangs up.

Right, where were we? Yes. Alan, the big fight.

He does a combat roll and hurts his back.

Amy, help.

AMY. Okay. So how's the date going? What have you two been chatting about?

MICHAEL. Favourite films. *Sister Act 2.* (*Gestures to* JORDAN.) *The Human Centipede. Withnail and I.*

AMY (*a lovely memory*). Oh I love *Withnail and I*. Do you remember we watched that together in that Airbnb in Minehead. Remember, Dave?

DAVE. Nope.

MICHAEL. Jordan actually said they wouldn't mind seeing me perform Richard E. Grant's final speech.

AMY. The Hamlet soliloquy? In the rain. Yes.

DAVE. No, no, no. Not the soliloquy! I'm about to fight Alan.

AMY. No, you're not, Dave. Help Alan out of this costume. What the hell are we doing anyway – how did we end up here?! Michael may well be about to die and we're hacking our way through this stupid play and eating delicious but totally unnecessary pizza. It's Michael's night! We're going to give up the stage to him and let these very game volunteers go back to their seats. (*Keeping the pace up.*)

Laurel, let's see how you've got on. Wow… that's really… can't quite think of the word.

DAVE. I can.

AMY. Can we please have a huge round of applause for Alan, Jordan and Laurel.

AUDIENCE MEMBERS *return to their seats.*

Scene Eighteen – Michael Performs Hamlet

AMY. Right, Michael. The stage is yours… for Hamlet.

MICHAEL *is about to speak.*

DAVE. Sorry to interrupt, Michael! I can't help but feel that you could use some music. We can use the underscore for Wells escaping the terrifying Morlocks.

AMY. No, Dave.

MICHAEL. I'd just like the sound of some rain.

DAVE. Too boring. Trust me. Here we go.

MICHAEL *is about to begin when Cher's 'The Shoop Shoop Song (It's in His Kiss)' blasts in.*

What?! So sorry, that's the party mix, where's the… hang on, I can sort this.

AMY. Put that sodding laptop down. I'll do it. Now, we're going to make it rain. (*To audience.*) Please, everyone rub your palms together like this. Thank you. Keep that going but I want the middle section of the audience to click your fingers. Perfect. Keep that going. Now I want everyone at the back to lightly pat your hands on your thighs, like this. Good. Beautiful.

She conducts the audience to raise or lower the volume of different sections. When she's satisfied, she gives the thumbs

76   THE TIME MACHINE

up to MICHAEL. *He begins. Then* AMY *fades out the rain. It is replaced with SFX rain.*

MICHAEL. I have of late, but wherefore I know not, lost all my mirth, forgone all custom of exercises, and, indeed, it goes so heavily with my disposition that this goodly frame, the Earth, seems to me a sterile promontory; this most excellent canopy, the air, look you, this brave o'erhanging firmament, this majestical roof, fretted with golden fire – why, it appeareth nothing to me but a foul and pestilent congregation of vapours. What a piece of work is a man, how noble in reason, how infinite in faculties, in form and moving how express and admirable; in action how like an angel, in apprehension how like a god: the beauty of the world, the paragon of animals – and yet, to me, what is this quintessence of dust? Man delights not me, no, nor women neither, nor women neither.

DAVE *leads the applause. He's genuinely impressed.*

DAVE. Whoa! Blimey. That was incredible, Michael. Bravo. Wasn't he brilliant? What a man.

AMY. Come on, Michael, what's next? Another role that you've always wanted to do but you've been constantly turned down for? Or a party trick? A bit of magic? Surprise us.

DAVE. Nine minutes until... well, you know... just saying.

AMY. Anything.

MICHAEL. Anything?

He looks at them both. They realise what he's saying. He walks to centre-stage and takes a position.

DAVE. God no, not *The Importance of Being Earnest* hip-hop dance mash-up. Amy, what have you done?

AMY. We're doing it, Dave.

MICHAEL. Let's do this.

MICHAEL *has placed out his hand ahead of him. Rap intro with the lines below introduced. This goes into 'C'est La Vie' by B*witched then finishes again on a rap.* DAVE *and* AMY *join in. The mash-up starts with lines from the play: 'A handbag. A h-h-h-h-handbag!' 'I am known for the gentleness of my disposition', etc., and ends with a big move and grand finale. Song ends.*

DAVE. That was...

AMY. ...unique.

DAVE. We *really* need that call to come in now.

AMY. How long do we have?

DAVE. Seven minutes.

AMY is struggling to keep the ball in the air.

MICHAEL. Right. Let's finish the play?

DAVE. What?

MICHAEL. Why not? The final scene.

DAVE. Of my play?

MICHAEL. Yes. At the end of earth's existence. We made a contract with this audience, didn't we?

DAVE. Okay, cool. And you know what, Michael? I think that *you* should play the lead this time – the time traveller.

AMY. You absolutely should.

MICHAEL. Okay. And I think he should have a companion.

AMY. How about Mary?

MICHAEL. Mary, yes. Companions.

DAVE. Wooh, hang on. That's taking some massive artistic licence right there. People are going to start accusing us of not being faithful to the source material.

AMY. Dave, the end of your play is too sad. Wells can't be alone watching the earth die. He needs a companion.

DAVE. Okay, answer me this – how does Mary get millions of years into the future?

AMY. Well, let's find out. Lights, David. Now!

Scene Nineteen – The End of the World

We're transported through LX and SFX into a very spooky future. MICHAEL (*as* WELLS – *the time traveller*) *is watching the earth die. It's strangely tranquil.* MARY *appears*.

MARY. Hello, Bertie.

WELLS. Mary? How did you get here?

Pause. DAVE *is on the side of the stage.*

DAVE. See. I said it'd be tricky –

AMY *mouths 'Fuck off' and points to the wings.* DAVE *relents.* AMY *and* MICHAEL *are left alone onstage.*

MARY. I'm in your dream. I'm your guide. Bertie, you asked me to inform you when we reached anywhere significant.

WELLS. And have we?

MARY. We've reached the edge of the map.

WELLS. It's blank.

MARY. It's quite a view, isn't it.

WELLS. I always hoped that going forward would somehow help me figure everything out.

MARY. You have to be brave.

WELLS. Maybe we could just stand here and watch the end of existence, the life of the old earth ebb away, melting back into the universe?

AMY *creeps in with Cher's 'Believe'.* MICHAEL *joins in.*

Scene Twenty – Michael Can't Accept What's Coming

DAVE. Michael? Two minutes.

AMY. God... is there anything else you'd like to say?

MICHAEL. Oh, I don't think so. I tried my best. Things are as they are.

AMY. What would you most like to be remembered for? Your proudest achievement.

MICHAEL. Co-founding our theatre company.

DAVE. Come on, be serious. (*Beat.*) Oh you are being serious. Is that really it?

MICHAEL. Yes.

DAVE. Your greatest achievement?

MICHAEL. Yep.

DAVE. Wow. That's... incredible. I'm genuinely really touched. Amy, are you also touched?

AMY hugs MICHAEL then heads to the table. DAVE tries to get in on the hug but MICHAEL heads towards AMY.

MICHAEL. Look, Amy, the phone hasn't rung – as brilliant as your idea was – and so I've probably only got moments to go. But I also wanted to say, Dave, that despite all the infighting and the disrespect and the fact that you've practically never listened to a word I've said or taken on a single suggestion I've made on any of our productions – apart from all that... you're the best friend I've ever had.

DAVE. I know.

MICHAEL. And so are you, Amy. I love you both, you know.

AMY. And we love you too. Don't we, Dave? Dave!

DAVE. Yes, we do.

MICHAEL. I just wish I had a little more time, that's all. Damn it. It's all about bloody time!

DAVE. Michael. Don't think I haven't been through this – getting angry doesn't change anything.

MICHAEL. Your great-great-grandfather and his stupid machine has ruined everything!

DAVE. Don't forget about Amy.

AMY. It was an accident!

MICHAEL. I'm still going to die.

DAVE. We're all going to die, mate.

MICHAEL. Not in like two minutes.

DAVE. Yeah, fair point. More like one now.

MICHAEL. It feels like my head's about to explode!

DAVE. Ah – that'd be a new one.

AMY. David!

MICHAEL. We have to get rid of that terrible machine and save humanity from itself.

DAVE. I'm not sure it's as simple as that.

MICHAEL. We have no choice. It has to go!

DAVE. Michael, no! You don't know what it'll…! Don't you dare!

MICHAEL. Arghhhh…

MICHAEL runs backstage and attacks the chair. DAVE follows.

DAVE *(off)*. No, Michael, no, no!

From off we hear their struggle and the sound of the chair being smashed up. MICHAEL *enters with bits of broken machine, as does* DAVE.

What the hell have you done?!

MICHAEL. I'm sorry. I know it was a family heirloom, but it was too dangerous.

DAVE. No, Michael. I don't care about the machine. (*He throws down the element he's holding.*) I care about you. Without the machine we can't go back. This will be the last time we'll see you.

AMY. Dave. The time?

DAVE. Ten seconds. Sorry, Michael. (*Beat.*) Ten, nine…

MICHAEL. Eight, seven, six, five, four, three…

AMY *and* DAVE *clear.*

…two, one?… One? One?

Scene Twenty-One – The Call Comes In/End

MICHAEL *gets himself into defence mode, waiting for the impact from somewhere.*

DAVE. What's going on?

AMY. Have we made a mistake with the time?

DAVE. No, no. This is always the time.

AMY *approaches* MICHAEL.

MICHAEL. Stay away from me. Have you got anything sharp, explosive or electrical on you?

AMY. No.

MICHAEL. Any poisons, chemicals or hazardous substances?

AMY. No.

MICHAEL. Wasps?

AMY. No.

DAVE. Michael, I think you might have done it. I think by destroying the machine you may have unlocked a paradox? Changed the outcome.

AMY. I've got so used to seeing you die.

SAM'*s phone rings. It scares the shit out of them. Huge moment.*

It's a withheld number.

DAVE *and* MICHAEL. Answer it!

AMY *does*.

AMY. Hello? Really? REALLY? Yes he is. No, it's all smashed up. (*Covering mouthpiece*.) Michael, it's a scientist. From the future.

DAVE. It worked? Thank you, Sandra!

AMY. Uh-huh. Uh-huh. Okay. Okay. Right. Okay. Okay thanks, bye then.

DAVE. Wow, you just spoke to a man from the future!

AMY. Woman actually.

DAVE. Sorry. What did she say?

AMY. She said that smashing up the machine would indeed have shifted the paradigm or something. But that… no, not paradigm, she used another fancy P-word.

MICHAEL. It doesn't matter about the word, what was the 'but'?!

DAVE. Polymer?

AMY. Nope.

DAVE. Palaeontologist?

AMY. Nope.

DAVE. Plasmodium?

MICHAEL. What was the 'but'?!

AMY. That our timing was out by a couple of minutes.

DAVE. That doesn't sound good.

AMY. And that it's vital you take a big step.

DAVE. Wait, what, *upstage or downstage*?

AMY. She didn't specify!

DAVE. Okay. Stage step or just a regular step?

AMY. What the shitting hell is the difference?!

ACT TWO, SCENE TWENTY-ONE 83

DAVE. I don't know!!

MICHAEL. How big a step, Amy?

AMY. Just step!!!

AMY pushes MICHAEL a step upstage. The set falls down around them. All of it. They're standing in the archways of the doors. They are safe. It looks as dangerous as it's possible to be. The actors should react as appropriate when things, undoubtedly, go wrong.

That size step seems to have been about right.

DAVE. Jesus Christ, that was close. Right, okay, can we finish my play now?

AMY *and* MICHAEL. No!

Lights. End. Music over curtain call – Busted's 'Year 3000'. (Begin from the drum roll in the intro.)

About Original Theatre

Founded in 2004, Original Theatre Company has toured extensively all over the UK, introducing Original Online in 2020, producing several acclaimed online productions. In 2022, Original Theatre was awarded a Critics' Circle Theatre Award for exceptional theatre-making during the Covid lockdowns.

Current stage productions as of November 2023: *Murder in the Dark* (touring), *The Interview* and *The Time Machine – A Comedy* (both at Park Theatre, the latter also touring in early 2024).

Recently staged shows: *Stumped*, Agatha Christie's *The Mirror Crack'd*, *The End of the Night* (a co-production with Park Theatre); *Being Mr Wickham* (UK & NYC); *The Hound of the Baskervilles*, *A Splinter of Ice*, *The Croft*, Sarah Waters' *The Night Watch*, Stephen Jeffreys' *Valued Friends* (a co-production with Rose Theatre Kingston); Torben Betts' *Caroline's Kitchen* (originally *Monogamy*); Alan Bennett's *The Habit of Art* (UK & NYC); Oscar Wilde's *The Importance of Being Earnest*, Frederick Knott's *Wait Until Dark*, Torben Betts' *Invincible*, Emlyn Williams' *Night Must Fall*, Terence Rattigan's *Flare Path* and the award-winning tours of Sebastian Faulks's *Birdsong* adapted by Rachel Wagstaff.

Online productions: *A Cold Supper Behind Harrods*, *The Shape of Things* (UK/EU only), *Tikkun Olam*, *The Fall*, *Miles*, *The Haunting of Alice Bowles*, *Viral*, *Apollo 13: The Dark Side of the Moon*; and a growing library of behind-the-scenes documentaries, Q&As and other exclusive content with Original Backstage.

Since Original Online was created in March 2020:

- We have produced 15 digital theatre shows that have streamed online.
- We are streaming to over 57 countries including America, India, Canada and Australia.
- Our loyal viewers have streamed our work over 54,000 times online.
- We have over 40,000 users registered.
- We continue to develop and produce for both the stage and online.

For Original Theatre:

Artistic Director	Alastair Whatley
Creative Producer	Tom Hackney
Digital Producer	Steven Atkinson
Head of Marketing	Emma Martin
Digital Theatre Manager	Aaron Weight
Production Co-ordinator	Lisa Friedrich
Social & Content	Paul Jennings for Hero Social
PR	Alison Duguid

Original.

www.originaltheatre.com
info@originaltheatre.com

About Park Theatre

Park Theatre was founded by Artistic Director, Jez Bond and Creative Director Emeritus, Melli Marie. The building opened in May 2013 and, with 12 West End transfers, two National Theatre transfers and 14 national tours in ten years, quickly garnered a reputation as a key player in the London theatrical scene. Park Theatre has received six Olivier nominations, won numerous Off West End Offie Awards, and won *The Stage*'s Fringe Theatre of the Year and Accessible Theatre Award.

Park Theatre is an inviting and accessible venue, delivering work of exceptional calibre in the heart of Finsbury Park. We work with writers, directors and designers of the highest quality to present compelling, exciting and beautifully told stories across our two intimate spaces.

Our programme encompasses a broad range of work from classics to revivals with a healthy dose of new writing, producing in-house as well as working in partnership with emerging and established producers. We strive to play our part within the UK's theatre ecology by offering mentoring, support and opportunities to artists and producers within a professional theatre-making environment.

Our Creative Learning strategy seeks to widen the number and range of people who participate in theatre, and provides opportunities for those with little or no prior contact with the arts.

In everything we do we aim to be warm and inclusive; a safe, welcoming and wonderful space in which to work, create and visit.

★★★★★ 'A five-star neighbourhood theatre.' *Independent*

As a registered charity [number 1137223] with no regular public subsidy, we rely on the kind support of our donors and volunteers. To find out how you can get involved visit **parktheatre.co.uk**

PARK
THEATRE

www.nickhernbooks.co.uk

facebook.com/nickhernbooks
twitter.com/nickhernbooks